I0839755

Book One
Hibberd – McCune Family History
1869 – 1903
By: Michael McCune

Introduction by
Kim (Dycus) Carr

ISBN-13:
978-1986207836

ISBN-10:
1986207838

4

Hibberd or Hibbard?

The earliest documents we have found on our Hibbard / Hibberd family begin in England. The spelling on these English documents shows an "a" for the correct spelling of Hibbard.

As the Hibbard family settled into America and eventually moved West, the spelling of their name changed to Hibberd with an 'e'.

This explains the two spellings of the Hibbard-Hibberd name shown in this book.

6

A Word to "The Cousins"

By Cousin Kim (Dycus) Carr

By "the Cousins" I mean our group of first cousins--Pat, Faith, Margie, Linda, Joe, Cathy, Chris, Toby, Julia, Georgine, Kim, Rob, and Cindi.

Only one of our parents' generation is still alive—Lucille (Luci Booth), who is just about to celebrate her 90th birthday this April, 2018. This means it's time for us to step up, guys.

We are now the keepers of the family legacy.   I feel confident that the family history is in good hands. "The Cousins" are a great group of people—resourceful and dependable.

For several years we have been concentrating on the Strotz side of the family but there is another side that is just as interesting and complicated.

8

This is Emma Monterey Hibbard and her son Joe McCune

Through these two people, the descendants of Susie Easton and George Strotz are linked with the McCune family.

The McCune family has been attempting to unravel the complicated life of Emma Monterey for years. Emma Monterey reinvented herself many times during her lifetime. In our family we called her Grandma Garrett. In the McCune family they called her Monte.

This book comes to us from Michael McCune, our recently acquired cousin identified by Ancestry DNA testing. It turns out that HIS great grandmother was also OUR great grandmother!

Michael's grandfather and our Grandma Susie were half siblings. Their mother was Emma Monterey Hibbard (Harper, Sneeden, Easton, McCune, Ogden, Garrett). She was one very complicated woman and the details of her life are next to impossible to trace accurately because of her many last names.

Michael has generously shared some of his family's photos with us and he has done a lot of work on putting together the puzzle pieces of Grandma Garrett's life. Here's what Michael has to say:

"We've put together what amounts to multiple chapters focusing on Monte and her immediate family. As you know it's difficult because there is so much to Monte's life (6 husbands, 2 or 3 divorces). Nevertheless, we are trying. Rachael and I have put together stories my mother wrote. There may be some truth, but I think these stories owe more to "Little House on the Prairie" than to reality. We'd like you to have Book One to add to your treasury of discoveries. When we get Books 2 and 3 completed, you will find the stories to be much more realistic and true to documentary evidence. We are still going through photos to add to Book One but figured we would send you the text. Hopefully we can give you a copy of Book Two and Book Three soon. To me, they are much more interesting than Book One."

Even taking these stories "with a grain of salt" they are still of value to us because they give us some insight into why some of our ancestors were the way they were. Life was tough in those days. For various reasons, most of the men in this book never seemed to stay in the picture for long. Some of them died young. Some of them ran off "for greener pastures". Some of them were not very nice men and the women threw them out. Therefore, this is a story passed down via the women, a matriarchal story, if you will.

These women were hard working, resourceful, and determined. They were not especially educated in a *book learnin'* way but had common sense in abundance. They were not dealt an easy hand yet managed to do whatever they had to do to hold their families together. We can recognize many of these traits in the subsequent generations that came down from them in our family.

Meet Michael McCune:

This is our Cousin Michael McCune, author of Book One. He was born in Portland, Oregon. He currently lives in Healdsburg, Northern California with his wife, Mary Lee. He met Emma Monterey when he was a child and remembers her as "a very interesting woman".

Michael's McCune's father, Joseph Lemuel McCune, was Emma Monterey's son and a half-brother to Grandma Susie.

Discrepancies

There are several things recounted in Book One that are not the same as the story that has been passed down through our family. The truth is probably somewhere in the middle of these two accounts but it's very hard to tell because there are few documents pertaining to the life of Emma Monterey Hibbard. By the time she came West and connected to the McCune family she was about 30 years old and had three children. By this point in her life she was probably well practiced in reinventing herself and at tweaking the truth a bit to make herself a more sympathetic character to others. We can probably agree that Emma Monterey Hibbard was born in Kansas on January 1st, 1875 and that she died March 29th, 1958, in Seattle. Practically everything in between is debatable.

I have a very vague memory of Grandma Garrett, as we called her. When I was 4 years old, Grandma Susie, my mom Sylvia Dycus, and I went to her house for a few days of deep cleaning. I was just the "mascot", of course, taken along because there was no one to baby sit me while Grandma and mom were both away from home. What I remember about her house is that it was dark because she wouldn't allow you to turn on more than one light at a time.

I also remember that Grandma Susie and mom, who were not shrinking violets themselves, were both afraid of her. They cautioned me over and over not to ask Grandma Garrett for *anything.* If you had bread at her house you could choose butter on it or you could choose jam on it—but you did not dare ask for both because she was likely to reach out and smack you. I kept my mouth shut and mostly sat at the kitchen table and colored the whole time. Susie and mom were both whirlwinds when it came to cleaning. They scrubbed that house from top to bottom while walking "on egg shells" so Grandma Garrett would not get mad at them.

Grandma Emma Monterey Garrett wore her hair in a tight bun at the nape of her neck. She usually wore a white blouse tucked into a dark colored skirt with a bib apron over it.   She seemed unhappy and more than a little bit threatening. Looking back at it now, I can see that she was suffering from some kind of dementia.   I am presuming that she was no longer capable of taking care of herself and we were there to evaluate that situation. She died a short time later.

Emma Monterey was never an easy woman to get along with according to both our family *and* the McCune family and this only got worse as she got older. None the less, daughter Susie always remained very loyal to her. When she died in 1958, Susie paid all the funeral expenses and to have her interred in the corner of her plot at the Arlington Cemetery. We know this for a fact because the receipt from the funeral home and the cemetery were in mom and dad's safe deposit box.

I digress. Back to the differences. According to Book One, Emma Monterey's first child, Ruth, was fathered by John Harper whom Emma Monterey refused to marry because he was a well-known philanderer.

Also, according to this Book One account, several years after Ruth was born, Emma Monterey birthed Susie (fathered by Thomas Easton) and next, baby Alfred, with a man named Al Sneedin. Baby Alfred and Al Sneedin both died in a scarlet fever epidemic. (Has anyone in our family ever heard of this Al Sneedin?) Their deaths were the catalyst that propelled Emma take her two daughters (Ruth and Susie) West in about 1904.

Contrary to some discussion in Book One, we are fairly certain that Al Sneedin was *not* Susie's father. There *was* a baby boy named Alfred who died young but we believe he was slightly older than Susie, not her younger brother as alleged. In support of this we have a Birth Certificate for Susie that shows her name as Susan Elizabeth EASTON born 09/17/1901 in Livingston County, Illinois. Her parents are shown as Thomas Easton and Monterey E. Hibbard. It also shows that she was the third child born to this mother. That would put her born *after* Alfred, not before him.

In some other notes that are in Sylvia's handwriting it says that Alfred was born in 1898 and died when he was about 6 years old. This would also make him older than Susie and if he died when he was 6 that would support the timeline for the move West in 1904, when Susie was 3 years old.

However, here's a curiosity about Susie's birth certificate. It was not recorded until 1946 and was based on a sworn statement from…(drum roll)…Monterey E. Easton Ogden. I know that Grandma Susie sincerely believed that her father was Thomas Easton.

Thomas Easton had been married before his marriage to Emma Monterey to a woman named Lucy Rilenge (about 1890) and they had 4 children together—Ben, George, and twin girls Viola and Violetta before Lucy died. Grandma Susie considered these "kids" to be her half siblings and in later years, called her oldest daughter Vi after Violetta Easton.

One more clue: Emma Monterey had an older brother named George Hibbard. George married a girl named Marion Snedden (note the different spelling) in Peoria. Obviously, there was some connection between the Hibbard family and a Snedden family so we can't totally discount the theory that someone named Al Sneeden may have been Alfred's father. Marion Snedden had several brother's, one slightly younger than Emma Monterey and two slightly older than Emma Monterey. Their names were Thomas, John, and James Sneddin but perhaps one of them had a middle name that caused people to call him Al? More research is needed on this topic.

Meet Nancy Randall Hibbard:

Nancy Charlotte Randall (*Chapter One*) was our great, great grandmother.   She was born in Clark County Illinois in 1857 to John and Charlotte Randall.   When she was a teenager she moved to the Kentucky wilderness along with her parents, brothers, and sisters. Their life in Kentucky was brutal and they moved back to Springfield, Illinois after a particularly cold winter when they nearly starved to death. Nancy was bitterly disappointed with her father's inability to take care of his family. This was just the first of many times that she would be let down by the men in her life.

Nancy married a tall, handsome, educated Englishman named William Hibbard. Nancy and William had four children: George, Emma Monterey, and Lewis. Then Nancy had three children who died as infants, followed by the birth of their last child Grover, who was 7 years younger than Lewis.

Nancy and William did not have a happy life together. William was arrogant, critical to the point of being abusive, and had a bad temper. Eventually he was committed to the County Insane Asylum after several violent outbursts where he threatened the children. William committed suicide not long after he was committed.

Meet Emma Monterey Hibbard

Emma Monterey Hibbard (*Chapter Five*) was our Great Grandmother and the daughter of Nancy Charlotte Randall and William Hibbard. She was a tall and attractive girl. At age 19 (perhaps 17) she became pregnant but refused to marry the young man involved. Surprising for the times, her family supported this decision. Monte had a little girl on 03/20/1895 and named her Ruth. *This* Ruth was Grandma Susie's older sister. Emma Monterey had two more children while living in Illinois—Alfred and Susie. Alfred died when he was young (about 1904) and devastated Emma Monterey packed up her two girls (Ruth and Susie) and moved to the Pacific Northwest to start over by claiming an abandoned homestead.

Susie Easton with Cousin Willy Hibbard

This is one of the few pictures we have of Susie Easton (Grandma Susie) when she was a young woman. The young man with her is her cousin Willy Hibbard. Willy's father was Lewis Hibbard who was Emma Monterey's younger brother.

My personal memories and observations

Grandma Susie (1901 - 1982), was left a widow with young children during the Depression.   She had to scramble to support herself and her children in whatever way she could. She sold eggs and "fancy" butter for cash, grew an abundant vegetable garden, nursed along the fruit trees and canned all summer to be sure there would be food for winter.

She was not a "warm and fuzzy" woman and some seemed to resent that but when did she have time to be warm and fuzzy? (In between milking the cow twice a day and baking bread?) Do you remember her EVER being idle?

Most times when you arrived at Grandma Susie's house she was either up to her elbows cooking something or upside down in the vegetable garden pulling weeds. (How did she weed that way without all the blood rushing to her head?) She would dust off her hands and smooth the hair back from her forehead, refastening the clip that held her hair to the side. She'd put on the coffee pot and pull out a tin of cookies (usually either molasses or peanut butter) and take a break with you.

The house was always clean and the meals were always hearty. She did her "wash" every week in the old wringer washer on the back porch even up into the 1960s when most of us were kids.   I believe that she found some degree of happiness (if not happiness, at least contentment) in her later years with Grandpa Ed Mitling.

Grandpa Ed was her third husband and the only Grandpa that our generation remembers. He was kind, funny and a great story teller. He was always pulling practical jokes on Grandma Susie, some of which backfired on him!

Up until Ed entered the picture, Grandma had not had great luck with men. Remember that she was drug around a lot by her mother, Emma Monterey, who is one of the main characters in this book. Emma Montereys mother had been repeatedly disappointed by the men in her life, starting with her father who drug them out to the wilderness of Kentucky and then "abandoned them there". I'm sure that there was another side to that story but this is how Nancy Randall (Emma Monterey's mother) *perceived* it.

Emma Monterey was a beautiful woman in her youth but she made bad decisions when it came to men, almost like she set herself up for disappointment because it was what she expected. She was a bitter woman by the time she was 40. When she came to the Northwest with her girls, Ruth and Susie, she was determined to succeed without a man. Still, there was a steady stream of men through her life— some of whom she married and some of whom she didn't. These relationships were usually passionate, turbulent, and short lived. This is the childhood that Susie knew.

Now a young lady, Susie married George Strotz and I'm sure she thought her troubles were over. George was a hard-working man from "a good family" of successful German farmers. She was NOT welcomed into the Strotz family with open arms, however. George married her anyway and they were well on their way to their own success with 4 kids when George died suddenly. His ambition was his undoing. In addition to working on the farm with his brothers he also worked at a sawmill. During an outbreak of the measles George got the measles along with "the kids". This was followed by a bout with pneumonia. He insisted he was better and went back to work at the sawmill too soon. He collapsed and died at work.

The next few years were very hard for Susie and her four kids. Those four kids are our parents and each of them had a different "take" on their childhoods.   Some of them saw the glass half empty and some of them saw the glass half full. I can only tell you that MY mother, Sylvia, was a half full kind of a gal. She remembered that they were poor but well cared for. She never had a new pair of shoes, but they always had plenty of food and a warm house. Susie was a good cook and there was always a pot of stew on the stove. Men who were "down on their luck" would come by the house and she would give them a bowl of stew and a piece of bread to eat out on the front porch and they would chop wood for her in return.   My mom recalled that she never turned away ANYONE who was hungry, whether they could repay her or not.   These men showing up at her house probably caused "some tongues to wag" in town and we must keep in mind that the Strotz **women**, in particular, never saw her as good enough for George in the first place and liked her even less without George to defend her. Susie's older sister, Ruth, also lived in town and they had a poor relationship.   Ruth and her mother (Emma Monterey) had never gotten along and Susie was often caught in the middle.   The girls grew up with a certain amount of animosity between them and Ruth *may* have enjoyed spreading a certain amount of gossip about sister Susie. At any rate, Susie's next marriage to Jack Murry Gardner (known as Whitey) was a big mistake. Whitey liked to "drink, gamble, and chase women". He owned a race horse and they spent one summer on "the circuit", going to various race tracks with the horse. My mother Sylvia was 8 or 9 years old at this time and remembers it as *"the best summer ever"*, but her younger sister saw it as humiliating and that they "lived like hobos". A lot depend on your point of view. To my mom it was a grand adventure and kind of like being on an extended camping trip. Some of them slept in the back of their pick-up truck and some slept in the horse trailer. They also set up a tent for more room and did all the cooking on a little wood burner stove that they could throw in the back of the truck when they moved to another location. This grand adventure to a child was probably a miserable amount of work for Susie. Imagine just trying to do laundry and keep the kids clean in this situation.

When Susie became fully aware of Whitey's gambling habit she started to worry that he would "bet the farm"— literally. Her little farm and house that she and George had acquired were her only assets. She divorced Whitey, which was a scandalous thing in the 1930s. Now she had a fifth child, daughter Lila, instead of four, to support by herself. Later on, Susie married Edwin Mitling on 08/28/1948. By this time, her four oldest children were all grown and gone (though none of them went far away) and only the youngest, Lila, was still living at home with Susie and Ed in her farm house. They were together until Ed's death in 1961, making Grandpa Ed the grandpa that all of my generation remember. He was tall, skinny, bald, always wore striped overalls and a striped cap. He had worked as a cartoonist for the Chicago Tribune when he was a young man and later as a surveyor and engineer for the railroad. He was a big storyteller and jokester. He was obsessed with drawing cartoons and every scrap of paper that came into the house was covered in drawings. Even the bottom of the card table was covered with his crazy characters. (I have some of these drawings and would be happy to share them.)   At first glance Susie and Ed seemed like an unlikely couple. She was serious and hard working. He was easy going and liked to have fun. I think by this point in her life, Ed was exactly what Grandma Susie needed. He would do silly things and she would say *"Oh, Ed, you old fool…"* and would turn away but you could see that she was silently laughing because her shoulders would be going up and down. She *pretended* to dismiss his frivolous behavior but I'm pretty sure she enjoyed it.

My personal relationship with Grandma Susie seems to be different than some of the other cousin's experience with her. Maybe this is because when I was staying over-night there was ONLY me so my time with her was "one on one" time. For some reason, she took it upon herself to teach me how to cook. My best memories of her all took place in the kitchen. My cooking lessons started before I was tall enough to see the countertop and all started the same way: dragging one of the chairs over to the sink to wash my hands then she would tie a dish towel around me as an apron. It was serious business and I paid attention!

Among other things, she taught me how to make an omelet and her instructions are still so vivd that I feel like I am hearing her voice and remembering it word for word whenever I make one. Her version of an omelet was more like a soufflé so I never order an omelet in a restaurant because they are just "not right".

Some would say that Grandma Susie wasn't a very affectionate woman but I think that depends on how you measure affection. For her, feeding people *was affection*, and do you ever remember being there without her forcing you to eat something yummy? When you were getting ready to leave she would always catch your face in her hands and give you a dry little kiss on each cheek. No use trying to get away—she'd chase you down and pin you under one arm while she delivered these kisses. If you struggled you were likely to get it more than once.

In this Book One, one of the "good guys" is Grover Hibberd. Grover was Emma Monterey's youngest brother. When she moved west her brother Lewis (Lew), his son Willy and her other brother, Grover, came after her a few months later and helped her get the place fixed up. Emma Monterey was a hard woman to get along with so Lew and Willy moved on after a year or so, but Grover stayed on for another year. Grover was Grandma Susie's uncle but he was something like a father figure to her because he was one of few reliable men in her life. He was easy going and when he moved on he did so reluctantly because he was worried about "the girls".   Grandma Susie stayed in touch with Grover all of her life and was grateful to him for helping to get them through a trying time.

I remember Grover because we went on a road trip down to see him and his wife, Belle, one summer. Dad (Dycus) hit it off with Grover right away because they were both big talkers. Belle needed eggs for breakfast the next morning so she sent Grover and dad out to the local chicken farm for two dozen eggs. They took me and sister Georgine along. Grover had an old coupe that was all round --no edges—and had lots of chrome. The suspension left a lot to be desired in those days and Georgine and I were tossed around the back seat as we bounced along the gravel road that lead to the chicken farm. On the way home Georgine was holding a big basket of eggs on her lap. Grover thought it was funny to drive as fast as he possibly could go and as he hit bumps Georgine was tossed so high that she kept hitting her head on the roof of the car. In her own defense, she had one hand braced against the roof and one hand on the eggs. When we got home most of the eggs were broken. Grover thought it was really funny but Belle was mad at him and sent him right back to the chicken farm *by himself* so there would be no showing off on the way home!

The next day Grover and dad took us kids out in Grover's boat. It was a smallish boat with a large motor. He cranked it up to full speed and we *flew* over the lake! Only after we got back did we realize that the lake wasn't really a lake—it was more like a reservoir and it was full of stumps that were just under the surface of the water. This time it was MOM who got mad at both Grover and dad because they took us out there without life jackets and Grover always drove "like a bat out of hell!" This is the only time I remember being around Grover but he impressed me as fun loving and young at heart, even though he must have been quite old at this point.

It's interesting to see some of our ancestors through the eyes of the McCune family. Their point of view is different than ours but many of the insights and conclusions are the same.

I'm looking forward to Books Two and Three.

Cousin Kim (Dycus) Carr

Book One
Hibbard – McCune Family History
1869 – 1903

by Michael McCune

28

The Moving Finger Writes
by
Mary Plotkin

"The Moving Finger Writes; and having writ,
Moves on: nor all thy Piety nor wit Shall lure it
back to cancel half a line: Nor all thy tears wash
out a word of it."

From

The Rubaityat of Omar Khyam

30

CHAPTER 1

Nancy Charlotte Randall was born in Clark County Illinois in 1857. When she was in her early 'teens, her adventurous father John Randall moved the family, which included her mother Charlotte, her brothers George, Johnny, Lewis and herself to the wilderness of Kentucky. They lived in a rude log cabin built by her father with the help of Charlotte, Nancy, and the boys.

The huge rock fireplace was the heart of the cabin. There were cupboards for storing provisions, a long plank table and benches. In front of the fireplace lay a bear rug and beside the door a rough bench held the bucket of drinking water, with a dipper hanging beside it and a basin for washing hands and faces. Charlotte and John slept at the far end of the room. Their big wooden bed was covered with a charming hand quilted spread. Somehow that colorful touch of beauty seemed to enhance the whole room. A wonderful handmade maple rocker, a gift from Charlotte's mother, complimented the furnishings. A ladder led up to the loft where the four children slept on pallets (straw filled mattresses).

The family found their new home exciting and challenging despite the hard work. Lewis was a delight to the whole family. He was too young to be of much help, but his sunny disposition and little boy wit made them all laugh in the midst of the most trying times.

The most wonderful time of all for the two older youngsters was when their father took them hunting. George was a sure shot, but he hated having to kill any of the forest creatures, Nancy had no qualms. When she looked down the gun sight her gun her hand never trembled. They never came home without some small game and the occasional deer that kept the larder full for some time. Charlotte's garden supplied them with vegetables.

They went to bed at night lulled by the murmur of the river and the soft sighing of the wind through the trees. They awakened to the lively sounds of birds chirping and the chatter of the chipmunks as they darted among trees gathering acorns for the winter.

At the first sight of daylight the boys would jump into their clothes, each trying to be the first to go down the ladder. Nancy enjoyed the few moments of privacy after the boys left, then it was her turn to splash her face with cold water, run a comb through her curly hair and sit down for the morning prayer before breakfast.

Money was running low and October came all too soon. It was the time designated for John to go to Louisville to look for work. Charlotte would spend the winter alone with her children until he came home in the spring. With plenty of wood and provisions they felt secure in Charlotte's ability to handle things. So, with a few tears and hugs and kisses, John Senior mounted his horse and waved good-bye.

Charlotte dealt with difficulties in housekeeping and cooking that seemed almost insurmountable, but somehow, she always managed. It was not unusual for her to be in the midst of kneading bread or busy at some other household task when the door would be flung open and two or three almost naked Indians would come striding into the small cabin. They would make unmistakable signs to show they wanted food. Charlotte soon learned that no harm would come to them if she offered them food, which she always did, quietly and courteously. The young Nancy glowered and fretted. Feeding the Indians was done with a great deal of sacrifice considering the lean larder Charlotte had to work with.

Nancy resented them until one day the Indians arrived with half a deer carcass that her mother understood was sent by the chief. After that, the Indians never came without bringing a brace of partridge, a squirrel or some other offering. Charlotte always reciprocated with a fresh loaf of bread for the Chief. As the months went by, the occasional visits of the Indians became less strained. While the three children watched, Charlotte began to communicate with them. One day she wrapped her arms around her shoulders and shivered. Pointing to the Indians with their bare chests, she asked, "Aren't you cold with no shirts on?"

The Indian, who had a very limited English vocabulary, stared at her uncomprehendingly for a few seconds and then a grin widened his usually stern looking mouth. He pointed to her face and shivered. "Cold?" he asked.

"My face?" Charlotte shook her head.

"Indian all face," he explained.

With winter coming, Nancy and the boys hustled to provide enough to last them through the expected cold spell. Nancy and her brother George cut down small trees and dragged them to the house where they were sawed into fireplace lengths. John stacked the wood against the house where it served to keep some of the wind from whistling through the cracks.

Not the least of their tasks was the daily hauling of buckets of water to the cabin from the river.

But no matter how rude the circumstances, children always find time to play. The two older boys wrestled and had mock battles. Teasing Nancy or four-year old Lewis was great sport. Nancy had no patience with their tomfoolery and was not above cuffing one of them if they got too obnoxious. Happy little Lewis loved the attention and took the teasing in good spirit. In the evening after the chores were done the children were expected to tend to their schooling, which Charlotte was very strict about. When they had finished with their schoolwork, Charlotte read chapters from books that she had brought with her that she deemed educational. Charlotte was determined to do what she could to educate them.

She was a quiet, gentlewoman, and to her children she was a bastion of love and strength. They adored her. But no matter how difficult the circumstances, children always find time to play and there was time for singing and merriment. Charlotte told stories to the children in the evenings with the heat from the fireplace making their rapt young faces glow. Charlotte taught them to read from the big old family Bible and they learned to recite verses from it. Charlotte also taught them to write and to do simple sums.

January of 1869 was ferocious with snow piled high. Shattering cold and vicious wind hurled itself against the small cabin and whirled the snow in a blinding blizzard so that going out for wood or to saw a chunk of meat from the deer carcass that hung outside the door was not only difficult, but extremely dangerous. Charlotte would not let the children go out any further than the wood pile for fear they'd get lost and be unable to find their way back to the cabin. She shouldered the responsibility of fishing through a hole in the ice in an attempt to stretch their meager food supplies.   No matter how Nancy or George, who was thirteen, begged and pleaded she would not allow them to help. "Only takes one to catch a fish," she'd say.

On a particularly cold day she had gone fishing and as the day lengthened the children began to worry. Finally, after several hours and numerous conferences they decided to disobey her strict instructions and go out to find her. They found her half buried in the snow, inching along. She had injured her knee and could not stand. Together the two managed to get her back to the cabin. When they got her into bed, they took turns warming blankets by the fire and wrapping them around her. It was a long anxious time before she stopped shivering violently and warmth began to flow into her body. As the numbness of cold vanquished, Charlotte's knee began to ache. When the covers were pulled back it was plain to see that it was dislocated.   "I'm going to ask you to do something terrible hard," she told the worried children. "You'll have to pull my knee back into place. It will be hard, and it will cause me a lot of pain, but if you don't do it I could lose my leg. See, it's already starting to swell. If you give my leg a little yank it won't go back and it'll hurt me just as much and you'll have to do it all over again. George, you hold my shoulders down, and Nancy you pull on my leg until you hear the bone snap back into place. If I scream, I'll try not to, but if I do, just keep on pulling." Nancy used every bit of her strength and when her mother fainted, she just kept on pulling, and then she heard the sound as the knee snapped back into place. The sweat was pouring down Nancy's face, and her legs felt as though they could no longer hold her. She knew that they all depended on her to be strong so she bit her lip to keep it from trembling and drew a deep shuddering breath of relief. Charlotte's eyes fluttered open and she smiled wanly at her daughter. The next day when Charlotte awakened, she felt feverish to Nancy's hand and her breathing was labored. Nancy knew immediately that her mother was seriously ill. After a hasty conference with George, Nancy decided they had to get help somehow and the Indians were their nearest neighbors. The responsibility on Nancy was almost more than her fifteen-year- old shoulders could bear. If she sent George out into the blizzard he could perish in the struggle to make the trip. If they didn't get help her mother would surely die. If she went herself, and was unable to complete the trip, then George would have to care for her mother and his younger brothers. "Please, God," she begged, "help me."

For the next hour Nancy wavered between determination to send George for help and resignation to whatever fate her mother must suffer. When Charlotte became delirious Nancy could stand it no longer. "George, you'll have to take care of Ma and the boys," she told him resolutely. "She'll die if we don't get help. Now don't argue with me, George. You're only thirteen and I'm fifteen and a lot more able to go out there than you are." Her brother kept shaking his head.

"No, George," she told him, "it's got to be this way. It's a lot of responsibility, but you can do it. The main thing is to keep the fire going. I know I'll bring help but-but, if anything does go wrong and I don't make it back it will be your responsibility to take care of things until Pa gets back. If-if Ma-" she couldn't go on.

The boys came to her side and the four clung together in a fierce embrace. Lewis sobbed while the two older children fought back the tears. Nancy went over for one last look at her mother and kissed a brow so hot that her lips felt as though they were burned. "Ma, oh Ma," she said softly. "Maybe what I'm doing ain't right, I don't have you to tell me so I have to do what I think is best. Please Ma, don't die." But Charlotte didn't hear her.

Nancy turned and smiled with a feeble attempt to reassure her brothers. As she opened the cabin door a gust of wind swirled snow into her face, and then out of the murky light two figures came into view. Two of their Indian friends materialized bringing provisions from the chief. The flood of relief was so overpowering that Nancy struggled to regain her composure. The Indians might lose respect for her if she allowed herself the luxury of tears. She led them over to her mother's bed and with a combination of signs and the few words they knew she made them understand how sick Charlotte was. Without a word, not even waiting for food, they left as noiselessly as they came.

The day passed slowly with Nancy becoming more and more alarmed at her mother's labored breathing and the temperature that was ravaging her. She kept thinking, what if the Indians didn't understand her? What if they don't bring help? The early winter twilight was falling when the latch of the door lifted and the same two Indians who had visited them in the morning came in accompanied by a wizened old man who was no bigger than a nine-year old child.

He brushed Nancy out of his way unceremoniously and with catlike grace made his way to the bedside of the sick woman. He pulled the covers back and laid an ear against Charlotte's chest. As he listened, the quiet was so profound that Charlotte's breathing filled the whole room. Then the Medicine Man went to work. He produced a skin pouch filled with a frozen blob of something and managed to make Nancy understand that she was to heat it. Nancy dropped it into the iron pot filled with water that hung inside the fireplace. The old man stirred it around with a stick until it softened. He indicated that it was a poultice, and that she was to transfer some of the steaming mess from the leather pouch onto a thick cloth, which was to be laid on her mother's chest. Then he brewed some herbs from another pouch into a tea and directed Nancy to spoon it into her mother's mouth.

All night long Nancy and the old man worked over Charlotte, changing poultices, giving her the herb tea and monitoring her every move. Just as the light of dawn stole quietly into the cabin, Charlotte started to sweat. The old Indian smiled and nodded his head. Then she started to cough and rather than try to tell Nancy what he wanted he got up and got a basin and just in time because Charlotte started regurgitating strings of yellow mucous in such quantities that it had to be pulled out of her throat when she threatened to choke. The crises were over and Charlotte would live. Nancy looked at the old man with a heart overflowing with gratitude. She didn't know any words to tell him how she felt. She knew that the proud old man would not understand if she threw her arms around him so she just looked deep into his eyes. He nodded his head and got up stiffly from the bedside.

Charlotte's recovery was slow, her brush with death was very close and it was almost a month before she could totter about the cabin for a few minutes and then she had to rest again. She hated her weakness and worried about the burden her illness placed on the children, but she could not seem to regain her strength. She lay awake at night and worried, supplies were running low and she hadn't heard from her husband since October. Supposing he had been killed, they'd never even know. Charlotte tossed and turned and her pillow was soaked with tears.

Charlotte's weakness frightened and somehow angered Nancy. It shook her to discover that her mother, who always knew how to handle any emergency, had somehow become a weak and vulnerable human being. It shattered the image of perfection she had built up. She struggled with an unreasoning feeling of contempt for her mother's weakness that filled her with guilt, and with a helpless rage at her father who had deserted them and left them alone in the hostile wilderness.

Nancy was only fifteen, but she was a big strapping girl of five feet seven inches, which made her tower over most of the women of her era. She could ride and hunt as well as any boy, and although she hadn't met any men except the Indians since they moved to Kansas she remembered the air of superiority which boys always assumed in relation to girls. She knew that women were supposed to look up to men and respect them, but her respect for her father had long since begun to crumble, and now she was overcome with a frightening loss of faith in her mother.

CHAPTER 2

In later years when Nancy told her children about that terrible winter and how they had almost starved her face became grim with the remembrance. Her mother could not regain her strength, and then Lewis became ill and died. The ground was covered with several feet of snow and was frozen too hard to bury their little brother, so a frail and emaciated Charlotte read a few passages from the Bible over the silent body that had been wrapped in a sorely needed blanket. Nancy and George fastened the body high up in a huge oak tree to protect it from predators until spring when the frozen ground would soften enough for burial.

The only food they had as winter lessened its cruel grip was an occasional rabbit or a partridge, and what came from the generosity of the Indians who were also suffering from lack of food. When spring finally came with its warming days everything seemed to get better. They could once again fish in the river and edible green shoots sprang up from the forest floor. Then one fine spring day their father came riding up leading a pack horse loaded with supplies. He was hale and hearty, and had spent most of the winter in Kansas City. Nancy was furious, and he got no welcoming hug from his daughter. When he questioned her, all her pent-up anger burst forth and her mother and father listened in amazement as she told him what she thought about a man who would leave his wife and children alone to survive in the wilderness while he lived in luxury in a hotel in Louisville.

"I'm not spending another winter in this God forsaken place," she said flatly. "You keep saying how valuable the land will be, well, it takes work to build a home in the wilderness and you want us to do it for you. If you plan on making a living trapping for furs, you can do it just as well with us living back in Illinois. Ma would never live through another winter like this, look at her, skinny as a rail and weak as a kitten."

John Randall was a selfish man, but he wasn't a mean one, and he knew that his daughter was speaking the truth although it rankled to have a female child as uppity as she was. Finally, John capitulated and the little family made the long journey back to Springfield, Illinois.

They settled into town life   gratefully.

John and Nancy made friends and soon it was as though their time wilderness was a bad dream.

Charlotte got back her strength and opened a small boarding house to help support them.

John   Senior embarked   on various   ventures, some of them made

money, but most of them didn't, so Charlotte's boarding house stabilized the family income.

The year Nancy was seventeen, a young Englishman fresh from England came to stay with them. Why he was there was something of a mystery, he was obviously a gentleman, polished and well educated. He was an Oxford graduate with a degree in pharmacy, which included quite a store of medical knowledge, which he shared with the miners who had various ailments peculiar to men who worked underground in the mines. He was not happy in his surroundings, and his obvious disdain for the type of people he was associated with didn't make him too popular. Like it or not, he was forced to work in the coal mines to support himself.

Nancy was intrigued with him, he was tall and extremely handsome in a patrician sort of way and Nancy found him fascinating. She was used to being pursued by the young men of her class, but none of them ever really appealed to her. Nancy and William Hibberd gradually became friends. She had never been much concerned with her looks, but she was a beautiful girl with large almond shaped brown eyes just slightly tilted which gave her face a bit of an oriental cast. She had a strong firm mouth and chin, but her lips curved sensuously. William Hibberd had never known a girl like Nancy and he thought her height made her look regal. He admired her strength, and the air of arrogance that stayed with her along with her disenchantment with the weaknesses of all the people she had ever depended on.

He had not been with them long when he came down with dysentery. Nancy nursed him through the ugly illness that almost took his life. When he finally began to recover he realized that in order to survive in this heathen country he would need a strong wife. He hardly thought of her in terms of love, she was too far beneath him socially for that kind of emotion, but he did decide to marry her. Nancy accepted him with some misgivings, he wasn't as warm as she would have liked, and his air of superiority with her rankled, but she thought she loved him. Charlotte was dismayed.

"Nancy," she said gently. "life is hard on women at best, you know that, and I can't see how you can find happiness with a man who thinks he's better'n you. A woman has to have a man, but the good Lord knows that you could have your pick of your own kind. William doesn't understand life out here and he never will. He's different and you'll live to regret it if you take him."

"I've already accepted him, Ma. I guess what I like is that he's different, if I have children they'll be smart like him."

"Nancy, honey, don't you understand? He's no smarter than a lot of other men, your father, for instance. It's just that he has had a lot of advantages. You don't take no pride in the courage and strength it takes to tame the wilderness. Your William wouldn't live through the winter in some of the circumstances we've been in."

"William wouldn't take his family out in the wilderness and dump them to starve to death, either, like your husband did."

Charlotte sighed. "You ain't never going to forgive your father for that, but what you can't seem to understand is men are different from women. Men are adventuresome, they make progress."

"Sure, they're so superior," Nancy mocked. "We wouldn't even be able to read and write if it weren't for you. You came from a family of some circumstance and you tried to educate your children the best you could. Everything we are, which ain't much, is because of you. All your precious husband ever did for you is sire a pack of children, half of them dead before they were ever born. If he'd been any kind of man we wouldn't have lost little brother. Don't you hate him for that?"

Charlotte was at a loss. "It near broke my heart to lose Lewis, but what you don't understand is that men are the way they are and women don't have much choice but to accept that. Maybe the Lord God has a plan we don't understand. John Randall is a dreamer, but there is something exciting about him. He isn't willing to work in the mines for some other man, or shovel cow dung on somebody else's farm. Nancy, you rail and fight against life, but things are, and that's the way they'll always be. You're going to have a lot of unhappiness before you get that through your head. Women has the business of child bearin' and it stops them from ever bein' free. They're beholden to men for their livelihood and the protection of their children. Your Pa dreams of striking it rich and if he did he would give it all to us. Most people don't have any hopes of things ever being different-----"

"But you do?" Nancy pounced on her mother her voice heavy with sarcasm. Charlotte winced so perceptibly that Nancy was suddenly ashamed. Uncharacteristically her eyes filled with tears and she bit her lip to keep it from trembling. "Maw, you keep telling me how beholden women are to men. You've taken in washing, kept boarders, sold eggs and brought in money for us to live on all along, and on top of that you've had all the responsibility of raisin' your children. How do you figure you owe Pa so much?

"I don't want to be beholden to anyone," she continued fiercely. "Oh Ma, why does life have to be so hard? I hate the way men treat women. Sometimes I hate life, I wish I'd never been born."

Charlotte was shocked, but at the same time a pain stabbed her as though Nancy's anguish had pierced her heart. She went over and took Nancy in her arms. Nancy had always been standoffish, and difficult to cuddle, but she had loved her mother almost to the point of adoration until that winter when Charlotte had so nearly died. Charlotte never understood why her daughter had become so cold and distant with her and it hurt. It was as though a dam of pent-up emotion had broken and Nancy clung to her mother, their tears mingling.

46

CHAPTER 3

Nancy did marry William Hibberd and she found that life was very much as her mother had predicted. After the first flush of passion and excitement had worn off William began to show his contempt for the pioneer woman he had married. He took out his frustration at the life he was forced to lead on her. In the first days of shared intimacy he told her about the big manor house in England staffed with servants. He told her of his life at boarding school and of the degree in pharmacy he had earned at Oxford. He described the big parties his family gave at Christmas time, and he showed her a picture of the proud looking aristocratic lady who was his mother. Nancy drank in the picture with a kind of wonder, as though she were looking at a creature from another world, which indeed she was.

He was going through a small packet of tintypes. There was one of a   beautiful horse with a white blaze running down his forehead.

"That's my stallion, Commander." William's eyes were so pain filled that Nancy looked away.

Then, she asked softly, "Why did you leave, William?" The change that came over his face was frightening. Nancy had never seen such stark bitter hatred in her life and his answer became a tirade.

"You don't think I came to this God forsaken country because I wanted to, do you? You think I was lucky to have lived the life of a gentleman? You think my fine university education is something wonderful? Well, all it has done is teach me that life is empty—ashes! I could not suffer like this if it hadn't all been taken away from me. You, in your ignorance, don't know any better. How can you grieve over what you have never known?   Every day I live is an abomination. Can you understand what it is to be a second son in a noble family? You're nothing, everything belongs to the first son and all you can do is hope he dies."

"William! You don't mean that!"

"You ignorant slut, what do you know of what I feel? He was as eager to get rid of me as I was to get rid of him, and he finally succeeded. I can never go back. He let me take the blame for something that was his fault, and if they hadn't got me out of England I'd have been hanged."

He paced up and down the room in near frenzy as Nancy watched appalled. She knew nothing of this man she had married. What her mother had said was true. He was alien to her and to the life he was forced to lead. He never spoke of his past life to her again, and she was afraid to open the subject.

He worked in the coal mines and though he considered the miners little above animals, he became their champion. The pittance they worked for, and the callous indifference manifested by the owners to the safety of the men appalled him. The brutal treatment of families when the breadwinner was killed in a mining accident was further fuel added to the flame of his hatred for the ruling class. He became obsessed with the idea that if the men joined together in mutual protection they could force the owners to give them better wages, and take responsibility for those killed in mining accidents as well as making them take safety measures for the prevention of those disasters which happened all too often.

William worked along with a few other men to form the embryo of what was to become the first miner's union. It was slow secret work, and they had to guard themselves against stool pigeons. Occasionally a known informer simply disappeared never to be heard from again.

William spent little time with his growing family in the years that followed. Every minute that he was not working was spent planning and organizing, but he provided for his family as adequately as was possible.

Nancy bore three children in quick succession. George was the eldest, then came Monterey and finally Lewis. George was stocky and strong and had a good head on his shoulders. He had a purposeful way about him, as though he knew where he was going and how to get there.

Monterey, a handsome girl, tall and lithe, had her mother's beautiful wide brown eyes and thick dark curling hair. She was headstrong and, Nancy thought wryly, not unlike herself as a girl.

Lew was cut from a different bolt of cloth. He was a dreamer, like his grandfather, and he looked like a highborn Englishman with his finely chiseled features, deep piercing blue eyes and fine brown curling hair. Even as a child Lew was extremely tall in an age when men seldom reached six feet. By the time he was seventeen years old he was six feet four inches tall without a spare ounce of flesh on him and was the constant brunt of jokes about his height.

Time had tamed Nancy, the loss of three babies as infants after the birth of Lewis was somewhat mitigated by the birth of Grover when Lewis was seven years old. The constant struggle to make ends meet and the necessity of serving as mediator between her husband and her children had taken a toll.

William was a strict disciplinarian. George tried to be what his father wanted him to be and bore his share of criticism stoically. Monte was his favorite, but he wanted her to be and act like a lady which was hard for her with her hoydenish ways and total disregard for the proprieties. Lew was the perfect scapegoat, he seldom had his mind on whatever boring task he was set to do and felt the lash of his father's leather strap more often than the other two. Nancy was alarmed at the increasing viciousness of her husband's attacks on the hapless youngster.

It was at this time that she began to worry about William's sanity. At first it was a little niggling suspicion which she pushed down in her mind, but as time went by and William's attacks on Lewis became more brutal and his expectations for his children more absurd, the worry settled over her mind like a dark blanket. It disturbed her waking hours and haunted her dreams so that she often awakened bathed in perspiration with a scream on her

lips. The next day she could never recall the dream or nightmare that had so frightened her.

Nancy tried to insulate herself against caring too deeply for her children even when they were young so that she would not spoil them. A perfectly run house and quiet well-behaved children made life a lot easier for her. Firm discipline from her was much better than the harsh punishment her husband meted out.

She didn't realize how vulnerable she was or how fiercely she loved them until one day when Monte was six and Lewis was four. She had sent the children after a jug of milk and cautioned them about being careful when they crossed the railroad tracks. She watched them for a few minutes from her kitchen door and couldn't help think what beautiful children they were as they frolicked along with their dog at their heels.

About an hour later as she was putting her churn away she heard the sound of running feet and got to the door just as Monte came flying up the steps calling "Ma! Ma," hysterically, her face grubby with tears.

"The train runned over him, Maw, and it cut his legs off. Oh Ma, you gotta come quick."

Nancy ran the quarter of a mile to the railroad tracks with no realization of what she was doing except that she was praying, "Please, God, don't let it be true, don't let this happen to my little boy." When she got there, little Lew was on the grass beside the railroad, covered with blood. His dog was beside him and for one horrified moment she just stared, with the sight swimming in front of her like some crazy kaleidoscope, then suddenly Lew was on his feet running toward her with the dismembered dog, now dead, in his arms.

Another incident occurred that summer that further made Nancy understand how deeply she loved her children and how foolish it was to try to insulate herself from that love. Back in those days rabies outbreaks were common and especially in August. One hot August day Monte and Lew were in front of their house playing when Nancy heard Monte scream. She got to the door just in time to see a rabid dog, froth foaming around his mouth, less than ten feet from the children and weaving right for them.

It all happened in a split second with no time for Nancy to do anything. Just as the dog was upon them Monte pushed Lew behind her and tore off her shoe, which she shoved in the dog's mouth. He veered off and ran blindly on taking Monte's shoe with him.

Lew always seemed to be the culprit in any mischief the two got into. On a hot summer afternoon when Monte and Lew were respectively ten and eight years old they were again on their way to get milk and Monte was carrying her mother's prize stone pitcher in her arms.

"Don't know what you're so all fired careful about," eight-year-old Lew was saying. "That there's a stone pitcher and there ain't no way you could break it." He picked up a stone and smashed it down against another stone. "See? The only way you could break that pitcher would be with a hammer and then it would have to be and awful big one."

"A pitcher is not the same as a stone, Lew. And if you dropped it you'd break it, and if it got broke Paw would whale us within an inch of our lives."

"It's a stone pitcher, ain't it? Stone's stone, Monte, and I tell you it won't break. Look," he grabbed it out of her arms and held it for a moment and then let it drop. In the moment that it took the pitcher to travel from Lew's hands to the ground the expressions on their young faces turned from frightened expectation to utter consternation. The big pitcher hit the ground and split into three pieces.

"Now look what you've done," Monte cried. "Maw'll kill you and she'll blame me for letting you do it."

"Don't cry, Monte, I'll tell Ma I grabbed it outer' your hands and it weren't your fault."

"But I don't want you to get a beatin', and what if she told paw?"

"Can't help that," said Lew manfully. "I should've listened to you."

"I'm going to tell Maw that a boy threw a rock at us and broke it, and that way she won't blame either of us."

"No, I'm not going to lie to Ma. I did it and that's all there is to it."

"Lew, you're crazy, you won't never tell a lie and you get a lot of beatins' because of it. What difference would it make? I don't understand you."

"I've never been a liar and I'm not gonna start now," said Lew stubbornly.

Lew and Monte were inseparable as children and George went his own way. One day Monte and Lew were riding along in the buckboard and Monte said, "Lew, if you promise never to tell, I'll tell you a secret."

"'Course I won't, what do you take me for. I don't go around tellin' no secrets."

"Well," she hesitated. "My titties are gettin' as big as biscuits," she finally confided.

Lew's promise to keep her secret was probably violated a hundred times or so. Despite the vendetta carried out against him by his father, Lew was light hearted and fun loving. He was full of mischief and loved to tease, a combination that came close to having fatal results.

On a hot September after noon he was plowing a field to get rid of the dry stubble and prepare it for fall planting, he was fourteen years old and always hungry so he decided to give the horses a rest and go up to the house for a drink and a snack. He got in the kitchen just as Monte put the final flourish on a cake she was frosting. Lew wanted her to cut him a piece and she wasn't about to ruin her beautiful cake by cutting into it before supper time.

He was determined and the two youngsters started to tussle. Monte held her ground, she was almost a match for her tall string bean of a brother. She made a run for the stairs with the cake intending to lock herself in her bedroom but he was right on her heels and managed to get his foot in the door before she could slam it. She set the cake on a stand and tried shoving him out of the room, but he was determined and he ended up pushing her into the little closet under the eaves and latching the door.

He went down stairs with his prize. He poured himself a glass of milk and cut a big slice out of the chocolate frosted cake. He polished off his mid-afternoon lunch in short order and then went whistling back to the field and resumed his plowing. Absent minded as he was he forgot all about Monte locked in her little cell under the eaves.

Nancy, who had been gone all day helping in the delivery of a neighbor's baby came home to find the fire out in the kitchen stove and no supper cooking. She went through the house calling Monte and when she couldn't find her she went out to see if Lew knew where Monte was.

It was almost supper time and Lew had unhitched his team and was in the barn unharnessing them. He looked at his mother absently and said he didn't have the slightest idea, and then his face changed to dismay as he realized that she was still locked under the eaves. He and his mother raced for the house and up the stairs. The day had been unbearably hot and the small space under the eaves would be suffocating.

When they opened the door, Monte was lying in a heap, her eyes glazed, they both thought she was dead. Lew lifted his sister out of her prison and laid her on the bed. "Oh, God, don't let her be dead," he barely mouthed the words. Monte's eyelids fluttered.

She revived faster than either Nancy or Lew would have believed with both of them putting cold cloths on her wrists and the back of her neck.

"Oh, Monte, I thought I had killed you," whispered Lew with tears streaming down his face.

Her first words were, "Don't tell Paw, Lew."

"Don't tell me what?" William had come up the stairs and was standing in the door.

"I almost killed Monte," said Lew brokenly, and explained what had happened.

The rage with which William reacted was frightening as he approached the fourteen-year-old. Lew stood his ground bravely. He watched in fascination as his father undid the leather strap at his waist. William drew back his hand to strike the youngster but the lash never landed. Nancy grabbed it in mid-air.

"You'll not beat this boy again," she said fiercely. "We've almost lost one child today and I'll not stand by and see you try to kill Lew. He was careless but he meant no harm."

William lunged at Nancy mad with rage, Lew ran to her side and George who had just entered the room grabbed his father's arms. The two boys managed to hold their father who was literally frothing at the mouth.

Nancy helped to subdue her husband and in doing so was suddenly forced to accept what had been trying to edge into her consciousness for a long time. William was not sane and he was becoming worse. His outbursts were getting more violent and Lew was in actual danger since he was most often the brunt of William's rages.

The family settled into an uneasy truce. William was still the autocrat and he forced Lew to go to work in the mines when he was still only fourteen. He was so tall that he had to go through the passages in the mine bent nearly double. He worked with a big German boy named Otto, who was sixteen. Otto delighted in pestering and teasing Lew. Lew was always slow to anger, but when finally aroused he lost all control. One day the heavy lad jumped on Lew's back once too often. Lew straightened up as much as he could, pinning the other boy to the roof of the mine and with all of his strength pressed the boy on his back harder and harder against the top of the passageway. When the other miners realized what was happening Otto was black in the face and nearly unconscious.

Lew was sick at heart, as much as he hated Otto he certainly didn't want to kill him and he had nearly done so. It frightened him that his temper could become so out of control. What if he was like his father and didn't realize it? The incident did win relief for Lew from the continual hazing and earned him the respect of the older men who had thought him something of a pansy. Lew could never forget the uncontrollable intensity of his rage, and along with that realization came the certain conviction that he was in real danger from his father.

Nancy's life had not been easy. It hadn't been any worse than a lot of the other women of her era and station in life, but the suspicion that her husband was insane was something she didn't know how to deal with. There was no one in whom she could confide or ask advice. Her mother was dead and it was unthinkable to tell one's friends. Insanity was considered a reflection on the whole family and definitely hereditary, so it followed that if the father was insane there was likelihood that his children would suffer the same fate.

She knew that sooner or later she would have to discuss her problem with the children, but somehow, she couldn't bring herself to do it. She wondered if sending Lew to stay with her brother would help matters and maybe stave off the inevitable.

One evening things came to a head, although, as far as Nancy could determine Lew hadn't done anything to incur William's wrath. They were all sitting at the table eating their evening meal when suddenly William rose from the table with the carving knife in his hand.

He walked around the table to Lew's side. "I'm sorry son," he said with uncustomary gentleness, "Your maw won't let me discipline you anymore and you are growing up with complete disregard for authority. I can't see that happen." He raised the knife as Lew looked up at him in stunned surprise. For one split second time stopped, no one moved. Nancy and George realized at the same time what was about to happen and George who was sitting by Lew sprang up and grabbed his father's arm just as he slashed down with the knife. The knife grazed Lew's shoulder bringing blood and ripping his shirt.

Little Grover started to cry and William looked at him in a dazed fashion as though he had never seen the child before. George took the knife out of his unresisting hand. Nancy's secret was out in the open, and there was no way the issue could be avoided. George went to the police and that night William was taken to the "County Insane Asylum," as it was called in those days. Nancy faced the loss of the main breadwinner, but even so her life was so vastly improved that she wondered how she had lived through the years of William's abuse.

For the first time in years she slept through the night, and after the first shock was over the children were bringing their friends to the house and living the lives of normal young people, but Lew seemed to have a more difficult time adjusting.

CHAPTER 4

Life changed drastically for the family after William was committed. Except for Lew. It was as though a black pall had lifted. Young people came to the house and for the first time there was laughter and fun. It was as though the old house had come to life. Lew tried to join in for the sake of the rest of the family, but his heart was not in it.

He hid his despair fairly well from everyone except Nancy. The first thing Nancy had done was to make him stop working in the coal mines, and surprisingly Lew left unwillingly. Nancy was at her wit's end. What was wrong with the boy? He had been the brunt of William's rages for years, it would have been understandable if he had been delighted to have his father out of his life.

She had a sudden inspiration. She knew how Lew had always loved his father's violin music, and she remembered the beating he had received when William caught him attempting to play it. She decided to give Lewis the violin.

At first, he refused to accept it. "Paw wouldn't want me to have it," he said, but he couldn't conceal the fascination he felt for the instrument.

For the first time a chink appeared in the armor which Lew had built around his feelings. Nancy took that opportunity to pierce his defenses.

"Lew," she said gently, "are you grieving for your father?" As unlikely as that possibility seemed Nancy was determined to explore it. When she got no response, she asked another question. "Surely you aren't blaming yourself for what happened to him?" Still no response.

She took another tack. "Your father had something terrible happen to him in England; I think it touched his mind. I first suspected that when we were newly married. He was never quite right. He hated everything about his life over here. He despised me for my grammar, my lack of fancy manners, the way I dressed, the kind of food I cooked." She had been sitting on his bed as she talked and suddenly he was up and began to pace.

"Don't Ma," Lew begged. "Don't open up all those old wounds. I knew that Paw wasn't quite, wasn't...." He stopped unable to continue.

"We have to talk this out, Lew," Nancy said quietly. "There is no escaping it. It would be a relief to me, too. It has been burdening me down. There wasn't anyone I could talk to. It can ruin your whole life if you keep on feeling this guilt or whatever it is that's eatin' you up."

"He couldn't help the way he was," Lew said miserably, "But I don't know why he hated me so when I loved him so much."

Nancy gasped. "You mean that after the way he treated you, you still loved him?"

"He was everything I wanted to be- fine and polished and clean. He wasn't like the other men we know. He didn't have to work in a mine with his education but something burned in him, he wanted to help the miners. The men looked up to him and he was a natural leader. A boy has to be proud of a father like that."

"Yet," said Nancy, "he despised the men he worked so hard to better, like he despised me. When I realized how he felt about me the love I thought I felt for him just shriveled up and died. Can you understand that?" She looked at Lew, her gaze mirroring defiance, anger and a fierce pride.

"I've never had any education, but that doesn't mean I'm not as good as that high and mighty family he came from. Our family left the comfort of the known and went to a new-world. It takes guts and courage and stamina to do that. All his family has done is lived on what has been inherited from generation to generation. To my mind that doesn't make him any better than me."

Lew listened to his mother in amazement.

She went on bitterly. "He made my life a hell and I'm glad he's out of it. It got so's I couldn't sleep nights." She put her hand on his shoulder and shook him gently "I know he was crazy and he couldn't help bein' like he was.   I'm trying to understand that and forgive him, but it ain't easy to do. The cruelest thing you could possibly do to me, Lew, is to let that hate of his reach out and snatch you away from me. You have no call to feel guilty. You are the smartest of my children and he wouldn't let you get an education. His excuse was that all his education ever did for him was to bring him grief.

"When you wanted to learn the violin, all you got was a beating. Lew, I want you to take this violin and learn to play it. It would ease the awful hurt I feel at how he abused and cheated you of the happiness that you deserve. Even with all that you could still be anything in the world you wanted to be. It's not too late."

Lew's eyes filled with tears as he realized his mother's deep hurt. "Maw, I don't really want to be anything special. I just want to end up married to a nice girl and have a bunch of young 'uns. I'd be good to them, Ma somehow, I don't think things will ever come out like I want them to, I don't know why. I just have this feeling. If only I knew why my father hated me so. It makes me feel like something is wrong with me that I don't know about."

Nancy put her arms around him and pulled his head against her.

"Lew, honey, I just want you to be happy. Albert says you're doin' good in the feed store. You went right to work for him and you never worked in a feed store before. See, Lew, you can do anything you want to."

"Ma I'll try to be what you want me to be, but when I think of poor pa in there with all those crazy people, shut off from the world and all because of me it near breaks my heart."

"But don't you see that it's not because of you? If he hadn't had you to take his hate out on, it would have been me or one of the other children. He was getting worse all the time and he would have ended up killing you and they'd have hung him."

"What if I end up like him? I would have killed Otto if they hadn't stopped me. Maybe I'm crazy, too. Maybe I shouldn't ever get married and hand that craziness down. All these things have been spinning around in my head until I'm near crazy already. Why do you think he hated me?"

Nancy knew that somehow she had to make her troubled son understand. She chose her words carefully. "Lew, honey, I think the problem is that you look like that brother of his that he blamed for ruining his life. One time when you were a little boy he was looking at you and all of a sudden, he said, 'Lewis looks just like my brother Charles did when he was a child.' At the time, I didn't pay it no mind, but now that I think on it, it was after that when he started pickin' on you."

"But Ma, that wasn't my fault."

Nancy felt a surge of hope. "No, it wasn't. That's what you have to understand. What your paw did had nothing to do with anything about you that you could help. He was burnt up by his own hate. If you were like him you'd be full of hate because of how unfair he always was to you. See, son, you aren't like your father and there is no way you should blame yourself for how he was. If you do, it you will ruin your life…… and that would break my heart." She put a finger under his chin and raised his face, looking into his eyes she felt that Lew finally understood.

Not long after Nancy and Lew's talk the family was notified that William had managed to get his hands on a piece of broken glass, slit his wrists and bled to death. Lew watched as the dirt covered his father's casket and a strange peace came over him. He was glad that William was no longer caged up and that the fires that had so tormented him were finally extinguished.

Soon after his father's death, Lew made a discobrty' He could play the violin! He didn't know why it was so easy for him and his family was dumbfounded when he came downstairs one night carrying the violin and asked them what they wanted to hear him play. With some amusement George suggested "Coming Through the Rye". Lew tucked the violin under his chin and played the tune. They named one song after another and Lew played each one.

One night at a dance the fiddler got so falling down drunk he couldn't stand up to play. The audience, eager to dance, didn't care who played just so someone did. The band-leader pleaded for a volunteer. There was no response until George pushed his protesting brother forward. The crowd clapped and cheered as a violin was thrust into his hands.

His first stumbling attempts to get into the rhythm of the band were short lived and the fellows covered his mistakes with good humor. When the dance  was over he got a big hand from the audience. The band leader was so pleased with Lew that he took him aside and offered him a steady job if he would accept some training until he learned the basics. In six months Lew was a popular addition to the little group and playing at dances all over the county. As he earned along the way he also discovered that he could play organ, piano and guitar which made him all the more valuable to the little dance band. He decided that if he was to be a musician he should learn the rudiments of reading music.

One night when he came home from work, Nancy met him at the door. He could sense her excitement. "Lew, I have something to show you!" She took him into the kitchen where some photographs were laid out on the kitchen table. One of them, highlighted by the yellow lamplight, was his own face.

"Now you know why he was so mean to you. It's William's eldest brother, the one he hated so. He was the one responsible for William being disinherited and banished from England. I'd swear it is a picture of you! I found these pictures when I was cleaning out some of his things. This is your grandmother, isn't she beautiful?"

Lew poured over the pictures, but he always came back to the picture that might have been himself standing by the young man who was his father. He studied the other pictures. So, this was the kind of life his father had left behind. The huge mansion, the magnificent black stallion, the mother with her jewels and her velvety, lace adorned dress. It was an eerie feeling knowing that he looked exactly like the brother his father blamed so bitterly. It was also the final release from the burden of self-doubt he had borne for so many years. His father's hatred had nothing to do with any fault of his.

CHAPTER 5

The next few years were probably the happiest of Lew's life. He had taken added responsibility in the feed store with a hike in pay. With the money he made as a musician on weekends and special occasions Lew was able to help his mother and had extra money besides. George was doing well. He had graduated from high school and was working his way up in a bank. Things were definitely looking up for the Hibberd family, but as is always the case, things never continue to run smoothly.

Nineteen-year-old Monte announced that she was going to have a baby. She had been keeping company with John Harper for some time, a liaison which was heartily disapproved of by the rest the rest of the family. John Harper was a rowdy young man, a hard drinker and a womanizer of some reputation. To Monte he was exciting, his wild handsomeness and an untamable quality about him made her pulse beat faster and ignited a passion that lit a fire in her veins.

"It's John Harper," said George angrily. "Well, he'll marry you, I'll see to that."

"He wants to marry me, George," said Monte quietly, "but I'll not have him. I found out he's been carryin' on with that slut, Jessie, all the time he was tellin' me how much he loves me." The despair as she looked at her mother and her brothers almost broke Lew's heart. "I know its unheard of for an unwed woman to bear a child when its father wants to marry her, but ...."

George interrupted her, "You're just mad now Monte, if you didn't love him you wouldn't have ...," he stopped at a loss for the right words.

"I love him all right, but what kind of life would either me or my child have married to a man who is never going to be faithful, who'd come home drunk from another woman's bed. I'm not just mad, I'm just not going to live a life of hell like Ma did with a man who had no respect for her. I'm sorry to disgrace you all, but with a father who died a suicide in an insane asylum I guess a little more disgrace won't make that much difference."

George who was on his way up in the world and was engaged to a girl from a good family could never forgive her. Lew's heart ached for Monte but surprisingly Nancy accepted her daughter's decision with a quiet fortitude.

"It's not the life I wanted for you, Monte, but at least you are meeting it with an honesty that is rare in women. We'll do the best we can." That was the end of the controversy. George's fiancée accepted the situation with good grace even though her family was shocked and somewhat dubious at the advisability of their daughter marrying into a family with such a tainted background. The fashionable wedding went off on schedule with Lew acting as best man.

Monte bore a little girl and named her Ruth. The child was adorable with big brown eyes, shining dark curls and a pert little face. Neither Monte nor Nancy would allow her to be spoiled, so Ruth was well behaved and actually a joy to the family. John Harper still begged Monte to marry him, and came to the house often to see the little daughter whom he adored. The family accepted him with varying degrees of warmth. After all it was not his fault that Monte would not let him do right by her.

Lew was courting a lovely girl named Laura and he was deeply in love with her, but when John Harper's sister met Lewis, his fate was sealed. She wanted him, and Elsie

Harper was a strong determined woman several years Lew's senior and quite a bit wilier than he. She had lost her husband in a mine accident and was bitter and angry about the hand fate had dealt her.

A gentle quiet man was calling on Nancy. He was a railroad engineer who had lost his wife several years before. He had taken a fancy to Nancy who was a fine-looking woman in her early forties. Nancy scarcely knew how to deal with the respect and consideration he showed her. They sat on the front porch swing in the twilight with the fireflies flitting around the gas streetlight and talked. Nancy had never really talked to a man in her whole life. They told each other about their former lives and she discovered that he had been married to a cold unloving woman. Both of them reveled in the companionship that neither of them had known could exist between a man and a woman. The icy barrier that had blocked Nancy's emotions for so many years began to melt and a timid love began to blossom. When Walter Hubbard asked Nancy to marry him she hesitated because of her children. He brushed that excuse aside with a smile.

"Grover is eleven years old and I'd welcome raising a boy,
 I was always sorry that I never had any
children of my own," he reassured her. "As far as the older
children are concerned, they are all ready to go about their
own lives anyway, and it won't be long before you're left
alone. Monte has a good head on her shoulders and when
a suitable man comes along she'll marry him and I'll hate to
see little Ruth leave us. You know I feel a real kinship for
Lew, he can live with us as long as he likes. Don't you see,
Nancy, if all your children wanted to live with us I wouldn't
care. You don't know how wonderful it is to come off a trip
and come here where your house is full of life and young
folk. They treat me like they really like me, and you always
have cake or cookies and hot coffee waiting for me—and we
talk. Maybe that don't seem like much to you, but it is like
a new world opening up to me. Besides, just looking at you
is a joy to me even if all those extras weren't thrown in.

"I love you and I want to marry you. I'll make a good
husband and you'll never have to want again. My house is
big enough to hold us all and the grand kids, too, and I own
it. Everything I have will be yours, and if I die before you
do there is my pension and it will take care of you for the
rest of your life." He was holding her hands tightly in his
and she could have no doubt of the love that shone from his
eyes. Quite naturally Nancy went into his arms. They were
married a few weeks later with the full approval of all of
Nancy's children.

CHAPTER 6

It seemed that everywhere Lew turned Elsie was there and she treated him with an air of proprietorship that angered Laura. Lew didn't know how to deal with the veiled warfare that existed between his sweetheart and the strange woman who was somehow insinuating herself into his life. When he got home from work she was there on the pretext of coming to see her little niece, Ruth. Wherever the band played, she was often there. She was an attractive woman and she never lacked for dances, but somehow, she always managed to go home with Lew. If Laura was there she claimed she didn't have a way to get home and accompanied them. Laura hated her and was as helpless as Lew when it came to dealing with her.

Lew and Laura had intended to wait a year or so before getting married, but they decided that the best way to get rid of Elsie was to get married right away. They had so much in common. Laura played the organ in church and had a beautiful singing voice. They both wanted a house full of children. She was right for Lew.

Laura never doubted that Lew would always make enough money to support them and send whatever children God sent them through college. When they had made their decision and agreed to be married in two months Lew held her in his arms and kissed her with growing passion.
Gently Laura pushed him away.

On his way home that night he rode his horse at breakneck speed hardly able to contain his joy. He couldn't wait to tell his mother the news. Nancy was sitting by the fire knitting and Elsie was there with Monte and John. Lew was dismayed, and he could tell by Nancy's tight lips that she was annoyed at Elsie always being there. Walter was on an overnight run and for a fleeting moment Lew wished for Walter's solid presence.

"Ma, I got news," some of the joy that had so filled him with delight had evaporated. He hated sharing his news with the two outsiders. He thought his voice sounded a little lame when he announced his marriage intentions.

Nancy was on her feet instantly, laughing and hugging him with open approval. Monte was delighted, too. The whole family loved Laura. John gave his hearty congratulations and said he wished Monte would make it a double wedding. Elsie had a frozen smile on her lips as she took his hand and wished him well. Lewis breathed a sigh of relief, for some reason that he could not define he was almost afraid of her, and he was delighted she was taking his announcement with good grace. He breathed a sigh of relief.

Several nights later Lew came home about four in the morning from a dance engagement. He'd worked all day before the dance and he stumbled up the stairs to his room so tired that he was taking off his tie and shirt before he got to his room. He undressed in the dark and crawled into bed numbed with fatigue. Suddenly he was wide awake. Someone was in his bed! As he tried to jump out warm arms entwined his neck and a soft naked body was pressed against him.

Lew was full of high ideals and the thought of a woman other than Laura physically tempting him had never entered his head. He would have had to be made of stone to resist the body that was twining around him and the hot kisses that were raining on his face, his neck, and his chest. Lew was not made of stone. He was a warm blooded passionate young man and he had never had intimate contact with a woman. Waiting for his marriage to

Laura was not without physical frustration. He finally fell into a deep sleep with the woman who was not Laura nestled in his arms.

When he awakened late on Sunday morning she was gone. He could almost have dreamed the whole thing. But it wasn't a dream and he was filled with a vague unease. He had known all along that it was Elsie even though not a word had passed between them. She had seduced him and to his chagrin he had been a willing victim. Why would Elsie do such a thing.

Should he forget about the whole thing as though it had never happened? Should he tell his mother? What about Laura, did she have the right to know? Every question that entered his mind seemed to somehow threaten his manliness. To say that the experience had not been enjoyable would have been a lie. What if she invaded his bed again? He cursed in helpless frustration.

He wrestled with his problem for three weeks, every day that went by made the experience fade a little bit more until he could almost convince himself that it had never happened and then the blow fell. One night as he left the store Elsie was waiting for him, she fell in step beside him.

"I've got to talk to you, Lew," she said urgently, and then burst into tears. "I know it's my fault and I can't blame you if you won't do what's right, but Lew, I'm in the family way."

"How, how do you know?" Lew stammered, aghast.

"Don't be a fool, Lew, how does any woman know," she said tartly. "You're the only man I've been with so you're the father, that's one thing sure."

"But I'm as good as married to Laura, how could such a thing happen?" Lew's voice was heavy with despair.

"You're not as good as married until you're married," said Elsie with an edge to her voice, and then, almost wheedling, "I didn't mean this to happen, you must know that. Lew, I've been in love with you ever since I first saw you and I couldn't let you marry her without ever knowing how deeply I care. That's why I did it. If it wasn't for the baby we could forget about the whole thing, but poor little mite, what's to become of it? How will Laura like knowing that a bastard child is growing up in the same town with her children? Think about it, Lew." And then she walked rapidly away leaving him with his whole world crumbling around him.

CHAPTER 7

Lew's wedding picture shows a grim faced young man sitting in a straight-backed chair while his smiling wife stands in back of him with a hand on his shoulder.

His parting with Laura was so painful that he never spoke of it and she left town soon after to live with a distant aunt. Nancy knew what cunning Elsie had contrived to get Lew and she despised her for it. Elsie got even by refusing to enter her mother-inlaw's house and making such a fuss when Lew went to see his mother that his visits became fewer and fewer.

Lew did not love Elsie, but he tried to make the best of his bargain. Several months went by and then Elsie took to her bed and announced that she'd had a miscarriage. Lew never knew whether she had ever really been in the family way. Elsie was a strange woman, given to fits of almost uncontrollable rage. She was so unreasonably jealous that Lew hardly dared speak to another woman, and then again, she could be so sweet and loving that Lew felt as though he was married to two different women. When he was twenty-four she announced that she was in the family way again.

Monte had married a nice young man and as it happened she became pregnant at about the same time as Elsie. Elsie delivered a sturdy boy on February 25, l901 and he was named William Thomas. Monte delivered a girl at about the same time and she named her Susie.

Lew adored the baby boy, but Elsie was so strict with him that Lew seemed always to be coming to his defense. When Willy, as he was called, was three, Elsie bore another child whom they named Veres after Elsie's grandfather. The baby wasn't strong and Lew worried that Elsie was not feeding him enough. Her tempers became more frequent and the two little boys often had bruises on their small bodies. Slowly Lew was beginning to see that Elsie was behaving very much as his father had. He tried to get her to consult a doctor, but any such suggestion brought on such fury that Lew was afraid to mention it again.

He lived in quiet misery, worried for fear she would seriously injure one of his little boys in one of her fits of rage and not knowing who to turn to or what to do. He thought about confiding in his mother, but rejected that. She was happy and it didn't seem fair to burden her with problems, which she couldn't solve any more than he could. He talked to a doctor and was told that Elsie was probably mentally ill but that nothing could be done until she committed an act of real violence. He finally talked to the police who told him the same thing the doctor had.

"You mean that until she murders one of my children there is nothing I can do?"

The officer shrugged, "I guess you could put it that way, but don't blame me. I don't make the laws. Anyway, we can't have men locking up their wives without any proof, can we?"

Finally, he turned to Monte. She had known that Lew was having trouble and had been worrying about it. She was still in contact with Elsie and they seemed to have a friendship of sorts, even after Monte married Al Sneddin and finally broke the tie that had seemed to bind her to Elsie's brother, John. Monte had three children now, Ruth, Susie and Alfred, who was a little younger than Veres.

"I wish I could help you, but I'm about the only friend Elsie has and I'm afraid that if I try to talk to her she'll go into a snit and there won't be any way I can keep in touch with you. Maw just treasures every little bit of news of you, couldn't you find some way to see her once in a while?"

"Monte, you tell Maw how much I love her, but there is no way I can get to see her. I work long hours and when I come home I'm always afraid of what I'll find. It was never meant for me to find happiness. I told Maw that a long time ago. Try to drop in and see Elsie as often as you can, Monte." No matter which way he turned he could get no help.

As would happen so many times in Lew's life, the solution to his problem was taken out of his hands. One day the youngster who lived next door to Lew and Elsie came running into the store where Lew was waiting on a customer.

"Come quick, Mr. Hibberd," the frantic youngster yelled. Lew didn't ask any questions, he tore off his apron and ran for his house. People were gathered out in front talking among themselves and the police were there. Lew was filled with a dread so profound that he could hardly make one foot go in front of the other and yet he was running. When he raced into the house Elsie was sitting in a chair with a wild look in her eyes, her arms and feet bound to the chair.

"The children," Lew gasped, "where are they?" A neighbor stepped up and took Lew's arm, "Willy is all right. Little Verie is bruised and there is a cut on him. He bled a lot, but he 'll pull through."

Elsie was bucking and straining in the chair as two attendants   came   and fitted her into a strait jacket. The sight of Elsie being dragged   away kicking and screaming would be etched on Lew's brain for the rest of his life.

Another   neighbor came out of the kitchen carrying Verie. The little boy held out his arms to Lew, and Lew took him and held him close trying to control the sobs that shook and tore at him. There was a blood-stained bandage around Verie's neck and a big bruise on the child's forehead. One eye was swollen and rapidly turning black.

Lew rocked the child back and forth in his arms, and he kept saying brokenly, "They wouldn't listen to me. No one would listen." Sobbing and bewildered Willy came and leaned against his father's knee. Lew sat down on a chair and pulled Willy into his lap. He sat holding his two children too shocked to think. The despair that filled his being was so deep that he thought he would never recover from it, and then subtly the warmth of the two little bodies against him began to exert their healing forces. Little Verie was alive, Willy was unharmed and they had taken Elsie away so the little boys would be safe. The flame of hope began to flicker.

Lew's neighbor told him what had happened. She had run over to borrow a cup of sugar —a life had been saved on such a small thread of chance—in time to see the child lying on the flood nearly unconscious and Elsie coming toward him with a butcher knife.

Kate O'Callaghan was a big strong woman but wrestling with the mad woman was no easy task. The knife sliced into Verie's throat in the fracas. Kate was bellowing at the top of her lungs so that several men who were passing the house on their way back to work after their noon meal rushed in and between the three of them they managed to control Elsie by tying her hands behind her and fastening her into a chair.

The days that followed were a blur. Nancy and Walter came as soon as they heard and took Lew and the two children home with them. They petted and spoiled the two little boys. Lew would come home from work to find his two sons sitting on little stools, which Walter had made for them, happily munching on an apple or raisins while they waited for their father to come home for supper. It touched Lew to see how genuinely Walter loved the little boys and how unselfishly he devoted his time to them.

Time worked its healing magic and Lew went back to playing for dances in the little band that Elsie had forced him to quit. They were in demand for weddings and big social events, but Lew never neglected his children. He got them up in the morning and when he was home he put them to bed at night. A year passed quickly, but once again tragedy visited the family. Monte's husband, Al, and all three of her children came down with scarlet fever. In twenty-four hours Al and Monte's baby, Alfred, were dead.

Monte sobbed out her heartbreak in her mother's arms. "Maybe God is punishing me because, God forgive me, I loved Alfred more than anyone in the world. I kept praying for Alfred to live. I didn't want Al or the girls to die, but I didn't think I could survive the loss of Alfred. Now it's come on me and I hurt as though I would die of the pain."

"Monte," said Nancy gently, "I don't know the reason but women just seem to dote on their son. Maybe it's because it's our only chance to be of importance and we live through them. Maybe that's not it either, but boys have always been considered more valuable down through the ages. I don't know why that should be or why women keep on letting it happen. It's not fair, but that's the way it is."

"Do you love the boys more than you do me, Ma?"

Nancy would not allow herself to avoid the question. "I don't think I ever thought about it, but when you were children I found myself giving the boys the best of things. And, yet, at this moment my love for you in your trouble is almost to break my heart."

Several months later Monte got a letter from a friend who had gone out west, urging her to leave Illinois and come to Oregon. Monte's friend, Sadie, lived in The Dalles, Oregon and she told Monte that right across the Columbia River in Washington was some land that a man had homesteaded and defaulted on. There was a small house on it. Sadie urged Monte to come out and take a look at it. Even a woman could file for a homestead. Monte sold her house and furnishings. She gathered up her personal possessions and she and the two girls, ten-year old Ruth and three-year old Susie boarded the train for Oregon. Monte never looked back.

Lew longed to go with her, but he was afraid to take Verie, who had never been strong. Taking him out to a country where doctors were few and living conditions difficult didn't seem wise. Nancy offered to keep the boys and let him go out and see for himself, but Lew would not leave his children.

He tried to visit Elsie regularly, but the minute she saw him she would try to wheedle him into having her released. She always sounded so sane that he would begin to believe that maybe she was well after all, but the doctors warned him that Elsie would never be well again and that it would be dangerous to ever send her back into society. Lew would leave with Elsie's pleas ringing in his ears. The ordeal became increasingly unbearable.

Nancy advised him against visiting her but Lew felt duty bound. One day when he went to see her, Elsie seemed different. There was a crafty look in her eyes and the minute he shut the door of her room she attacked him with such obvious intent to kill that Lew found himself fighting for his life. Her strength was overwhelming. If she had possessed a weapon he would not have escaped alive.

When an attendant finally heard him calling for help he was bleeding, scratched and bitten. He talked with the doctor while his wounds were treated.

"Lew," said the doctor kindly. "I know you mean well, but don't come to see Elsie any more. You can't help her and you upset her so that she is even more difficult to handle. You give her hope that she might get out, and she plans how to accomplish it through you. Unfortunately, she blames you for all her troubles. She has a kind of mania for which there is no known cure, she'll have to spend the rest of her life with us, and it is likely she'll live a long life. There is nothing life threatening about her disease."

"You mean she will live her whole life here? Oh my God! What is it about me? My father died right in this building because of me, and now I've driven Elsie to this?"

The doctor looked at Lew in surprise. Suddenly his expression changed to anger and frustration and he lashed out at Lew harshly. "Don't be a damn fool, Lew. Your wife and your father both were unfortunately inflicted with mental disease. I hope you have more sense than to spend the rest of your life wallowing in self-pity and unfounded guilt. You should take your children and get out of this state, start a new life and forget that Elsie ever existed. She told me how she had tricked you into marrying her, it would have been funny had it not been so tragic. If there is a victim in this mess it is you. Now, you'd better pull yourself together and accept the fact that your only fault was in being such an easy mark. You owe your sons a man for a father and not a sniveling incompetent who wallows in his manufactured guilt.

"And let me tell you something else, young man. There will be times in your life when you will feel guilty about something you've done. Make restitution if you can and then forget it. As for self-inflicted undeserved guilt, I have no patience with that. The real name for that is selfpity with a big dose of the martyr thrown in."

The words stung Lew like whiplashes, but they freed him. He never forgot the doctor's words and they stood him in good stead in the years that followed. When he told his mother about the conversation later she patted his hand. "God bless that wise man" she said simply.

Lew thought a lot about the doctor's advice to leave Illinois. Things were easy for him now, but what would it be like for his children to grow up in a town where their mother was an inmate of an insane asylum? If he went someplace else would he need to tell the youngsters? Once again, the decision was taken out of his hands.

The winter of 1906 was bitter and scarlet Fever, Diphtheria and pneumonia harvested more than their usual quota. Veres and Willy came down with Scarlet Fever at the same time. The following night as an exhausted Lew lay catnapping on the bed with a gravely ill child on either side of him, a presence came to him. Lew could never fully explain the visitation except to say that it was there and he was made to understand that one of his sons would die and the power was given to him to make the choice as to which one it would be. He wrestled with the problem in anguish. Three-year-old Verie was a beautiful child with a sunny disposition and everyone loved him. Lew confessed to himself in his lonely vigil that he was partial to the little one. Six-year-old Willy was hard headed and stubborn, and hard to handle, but he was much bigger and stronger for his age. He wasn't as sensitive as his gentle little brother and probably wouldn't suffer the adversities of life as deeply as Verie would.

"Don't make me do this," Lew begged silently, but the pesence was gone. He was holding Verie's hot little foot in his hand and with a breaking heart he made his decision. If he had to lose one of them it had better be delicate little Verie. Even as he made his choice the little boy's foot cooled, and as the heat left the tiny body his little son's life ebbed away.

CHAPTER 8

The Dalles was a teeming mini-metropolis along the Columbia River in a country of vast spaces where farms and ranches and lumber mills were being carved out of the wilderness. Sadie Morgan met them at the train. The friendship between Monte and Sadie was deep and long standing.

Sadie assured Monte that the homestead across the river in Washington was still available and could be had for very little money. Monte was thrilled and excited. The possibility of owning her own land was all she could think of. Sadie took Monte and the children across the Columbia River on the ferry and headed for the high country on the Washington side. Sadie had a friend who lived on High Prairie and she was sure Monte would like the country. The team toiled up the rutted roads until they got to a plateau, a vast flat expanse of wheat land.

"There's a place down at the end of the road where you drop down off the prairie, I only hope I can find it. An old guy settled down there and built a house, but he never filed on the place. I thought about getting it for myself, but I like city life. I'll just show it to you." Sadie flicked the buggy whip and the horses broke into a trot. For several miles, they jogged along through the flatland and almost abruptly they came to the end of the prairie and the road suddenly started straight down.

They wended their way through thick timber down a road so rutted that the horses had to pick their way carefully. The buggy jolted and bumped and the four passengers had to hang on for dear life. Sadie reined the horses to a stop. Monte raised her eyes from her tense preoccupation with whether the buggy could negotiate the road without turning over. Her heart missed a beat and seemed to flutter in her chest, so great was the feeling that swept over her.

Straight across from them to the Northwest, rising out of a sea of green forests mighty Mount Adams pushed its massive shoulders into the heavens. Its snowy peak sparkled whitely against the vivid blue sky.

Monte drew a shivering breath. "I've come home, Sadie," she said quietly. Monte had scrambled down from the buggy and was surveying her new home before the others were on the ground. Monte walked over to the house that was built on a hillside. There was a room built into the earth under the house. My root cellar breathed Monte happily.

"What in the world is a root cellar?" asked a thoroughly disenchanted Ruth.

"It's a place where I'll store the root vegetables for winter that I'll grow in my garden. I'll can tons of vegetables and store flour and sugar and oatmeal and all the staples and I'll..."

An outraged daughter interrupted her enthusiastic mother sharply. "You don't really think we are going to live here'" she interrupted in shocked dismay.

When they opened the door to the house a couple of squirrels scurried out through a broken window pane and mice scampered to their various hiding places. Ruth bursts into tears. "I won't live here she sobbed. "I hate it here, I want to go home." Little Susie sucked her thumb and regarded her future home impassively. The house was less than 700 square feet in size. It was square, with a kitchen and living room cutting it in two-thirds. A long narrow room ran across the back of the house, sharing the other third with an open porch built over the root cellar.

Monte was filled with delight. Her busy mind was placing furniture. The long room beside the open porch would do for a bedroom. There was probably just enough room for two full beds with a walkway in between. She never could figure out what the porch was for except that it was the only place in the house from which Mount Adams could be seen. There were no windows on the West Side of the house. She marveled at the huge old oak tree that. It grew across from the root cellar and loomed at least twenty feet above the top of the house.

She went back outside and drank in the beauty of the setting that she knew was to be her home. "I'll Clear off that area down there for my garden," she breathed. "And I'll plant fruit trees and berry bushes and I'll put a barn right there...."

"Lord, Monte," Sadie gave her friend a speculative look. "I believe you'll do it. Anyone else, I'd say they were crazy, but you'll do it."

Monte filed for the papers to her homestead and proceeded to make a home for herself in what was literally untamed wilderness. The neighbors complained that Monte killed so many rattlesnakes that they were leaving her place and moving to their farms. The snakes were so numerous that one morning when Monte went to punch down her bread dough rising in a crock by the kitchen stove she found a big Diamondback rattler curled up on top the covered dough.

She cleared enough ground to plant a small garden, she fixed the windowpanes in her house and she shopped for the barest essentials in furnishings. She cut down trees and sawed firewood and stacked it against the house for the coming winter. She did everything herself except for grudgingly hiring a couple of men to dig a cistern to catch rain water and melting snow during the winter and spring to last through the dry summer months. There was no other source of water on the place. The men built her an outside privy and plowed up ground for her garden. Monte paid them with a sinking heart. She was running low on money.

Ruth and Susie spent some of their time with Sadie. When they were at home with Monte she had little time to spend with them, and Ruth was saddled with the care of her little sister along with other chores including keeping a fire going in the kitchen stove and enough water on the beans to keep them from burning.

Monte worked from dawn until dark, and she had little sympathy for her recalcitrant daughter. She was making a home for them against almost insurmountable odds.

A kind of fierce ecstasy burned in Monte. This was her land, no one could ever take it away from her and she loved it with a consuming passion. Summer faded into fall and Monte was ready for the coming winter. She had harvested beans, potatoes, squash and carrots from her garden despite the shortage of water and her never ending war with bugs, deer and rabbits. It was painful to see a deer munching on her Swiss- chard. Feeding her little family was not going to be a problem this year, but she wondered how she would get along when her fast diminishing nest egg was gone. She thought it would last another year, maybe two if she was very careful and then what? She brushed the worry from her mind.

There were so many things she had to buy. She needed a horse and a light wagon, and she had to build some kind of lean-to to shelter the horse in the winter. But no hurdle was too high to jump. Nothing seemed to dampen her faith in her future. For the first time in her life she was free! She did what she pleased, and what she pleased was to get up at day break and work until sun down, fall in bed exhausted at night and start the next grueling day all over again.

Back in Illinois she had dressed in the latest fashion, her hair neatly coifed. Her dark eyes contrasted against the whiteness of her satin skin. She was a beautiful woman and she knew it. Now her skin was a golden brown and her dark curls were either braided or pinned back from her face in a knot. She had taken to wearing men's pants to work despite Ruth's outraged protests.

When winter came, as Sadie had warned her, they were snowed in. Monte remembered the winter back in Kentucky that her mother told her about. Monte had no intention of either starving or freezing to death.

She had stacks of wood. The cupboards that she had the workmen build were stocked with lard, beans, flour, rice, baking powder, sugar, molasses, canned milk and oatmeal to name a few of the staples. Down in the root cellar were potatoes, carrots, apples, cabbages and several slabs of bacon. She breathed a sigh of exultation.

Monte had brought a stack of books from Illinois and Sadie loaned her more. Out in the privy were mail order catalogues to pour over. There was plenty of reading material, including the family Bible, to get them through the long winter evenings.

Monte was an inspired story-teller and she told them of the winter their grandmother had suffered through. "We come of hardy pioneer people," she told them proudly.

"But they didn't have to stay there forever," Ruth protested.

One morning Monte awakened and went to the door to look out. The sight that met her eyes was so beautiful, so unreal that it was eerie. The ground was completely carpeted in white. It had snowed in the night and big soft flakes clung to every leaf, every bush, and every tree branch. The whole world was a gleaming, sparkling fairyland, completely soundless.

The little family got through the winter surprisingly well. Ruth read every single book in the house from cover to cover and then tackled the family Bible. Ruth was an exceedingly bright youngster, and Monte was proud of her. However, Ruth and Monte were always at cross-purposes. Monte had decided that as soon as spring came she'd send Ruth to the little one room school that was about four miles away. She sighed, she'd have to see about getting a pony for Ruth to ride, and she'd need a horse for clearing the land and plowing. She had no idea how she'd get the horses, but somehow, she'd have to manage.

During the winter Monte had become a part of the

small community of hard-working farmers and their wives who were her neighbors.

The young widow and her two children were welcomed into the little community and whenever there was

a social gathering a sleigh would come down the road to pick up Monte and the girls. They had parties and dances and a Christmas celebration. The old-fashioned hoe-downs went on past day break with a tall thin hook-nosed man playing the fiddle for the square dances. A serious round bellied autocrat called out the changes. He wasn't the least bit shy about holding up his hand to stop the fiddle and roundly castigating any miscreant who was too stupid, drunk or inept to follow his directions. Monte thought of Lew and how he could make a fiddle sing.

There were a number of single men looking for wives and Monte could have had her pick of any of them, but she was reluctant to surrender her freedom. At one of the dances she saw a tall tanned young man with a crop of shining black curls, and for no understandable reason she felt a strange excitement quicken the blood in her veins.

When he danced with her there was no denying the chemistry that existed between them. Monte knew that he would come to see her. All the next day she thought about him and she remembered that the same spark had existed between her and John Harper. She vowed that if Joe McCune wanted her he'd have to marry her.

92

CHAPTER 9

Marriage to Monte, who was the mother of two children, was not on Joe's agenda. When he married it would have to be a younger woman who was a virgin. He told that to Monte once when their stormy courtship erupted into another of their bitter battles.

"Why would I want to marry you?" he asked brutally. "You've belonged to two other men. I don't see why you keep denying what's between us, what have you got to lose anyway?"

Monte's face paled with anger, and suddenly Joe's desire for the proud independent woman was more than he could bear. He grabbed her and pulled her into his arms and covered her face with kisses. He tried to throw her onto the front room couch, but she wriggled out of his grasp and before he knew what she was about, she grabbed her shot gun which was standing against the wall and he found himself looking down the barrel.

"Come on now, Monte, you know that guns not loaded. You trying to scare me?" He took a step forward and heard the click of the hammer as she pulled it back. "My God, Monte what are you doing?"

"I'm fixing to kill you," she said calmly, but with a cold implacability. "If you want to find out whether this gun is loaded," she taunted, "just take one more step toward me. Now you scum, get off my place and don't you ever step foot on it again. If you do, I'll blow your head off. Is that clear?" Her eyes were hard and steely and Joe didn't doubt for a moment that she meant what she said. He felt like an utter fool as he mounted his horse and rode away.

Monte threw herself into her work with a vengeance, too tired at night to even think about Joe as she worked to build a shelter for the horse she planned to buy in the spring. She worked in several feet of snow, her hands almost too numb with cold to hammer the nails straight. Sometimes at night she would awaken shaking with anger because of her weakness in allowing Joe to invade her dreams.

She became acquainted with the Klickitat Indians that spring. The old chief would come riding up on his pony, sometimes with a wife, or with one of his many children, and sometimes alone. The chief spoke some English and Monte loved questioning him and learning about the lives of the Indians. They were a short squat people and there was always the smell of fish about them. The chief often brought a gift of a big steelhead salmon, a grouse or a pheasant, and she'd give him a loaf of bread or some of the hot rolls he so dearly loved if she was baking.

On one of his visits he brought a pinto pony that he said was too small to be of much account, but would be fine for her girl to ride to school. Monte had told him about her need and she could scarcely believe him when he offered her the colt for ten dollars. She bought it on the spot. Now Ruth could go to school on a regular basis. Then one of her neighbors kindly gave her the use of a mare that was with foal and not fit for hard work, but would be fine for the kind of light jobs that Monte would use her for. The foal would, of course, go back to the neighbor when it was old enough. Monte could scarcely believe her good fortune.

The hot summer went by and the cistern ran low, but Monte's garden thrived. Several summer rains fell on the thirsty ground and her berry bushes and her young fruit trees flourished. Monte pictured jars of peaches and cherries, boxes of apples and raspberry and loganberry jam filling her shelves in the years to come.

She got down on her knees at night and thanked God for his beneficence, but for all her joy at being independent and obligated to no man, there was an empty ache in her heart that wouldn't go away. Her physical yearning translated into dreams with ecstasy flooding through her body and awakening her at its peak. She buried her guilt at the primal longing that she could not control in hard backbreaking work.

One fall afternoon Monte was working in her garden attired in a dilapidated shirt, pants and boots. Her hair was jammed under an old felt hat so that only a few curls escaped and had to be constantly brushed back leaving a dirty smear across her forehead. She was so engrossed in her work that she hadn't heard the horse approach and when it stopped a few feet from her she looked up. There sat Joe McCune.

They regarded each other for a few minutes without speaking. Joe was dismayed at her appearance, and yet she had never looked more desirable. Monte thought he was the handsomest man she had ever seen, but the aura of danger made her harden her heart.

"I've come to marry you," he said, as though he had to force the words out.

For one astonished moment Monte looked at him, and then a flood of anger so violent washed over her that she was literally speechless. She raised her hoe and would have slashed him if he hadn't reined his horse back and jumped off almost in one motion. Before she could recover from his surprise maneuver he grabbed both of her hands in his and the hoe clattered to the ground.

"God, Monte, you are so beautiful and exciting when you're mad. No wonder I can't stay away from you." He pulled her toward him impervious to her rigid resistance.

Monte found her voice, as she struggled out of his grasp. She was so outraged that the words tumbled out in a stuttering avalanche. "You conceited ass, you've got more nerve than any one human being is entitled to. You think all you have to do is come here and promise to marry me and I'll fall into your arms overcome with joy." Her voice sputtered to a stop.

"Monte, don't fight me," he was actually pleading. "I'm licked. I've hungered for you day and night. I've stayed away because it scares me to think of marrying a woman I can't get along with. But it's no use. A feeling like this only comes once in a lifetime, and I know I'll never have a moment's peace until you're mine. Don't you think we could get along in double harness if we tried?"

They were married in The Dalles, Oregon the next day. Sadie Gordon took the girls for two weeks so the young couple could have a honeymoon. For the first ten days, their lovemaking was a conflagration that threatened to consume them, but other than their passion they didn't have much to say to each other. His attitude after they had made love was strange, somehow, she got the feeling that he didn't quite approve of her ardor.

His home was in southeastern Oregon, and he only came to Washington on cattle buying or horse trading trips. He was reluctant to talk about his life, or to make any plans for their future. He did tell her that he had been raised by his three older sisters who were all school-teachers.

Monte was beset with misgivings. She hated his superior attitude in relation to her. He ordered her about as though she were a serving maid and showed no appreciation for the fact that on what was supposed to be their honeymoon they were staying at her home and she was doing the cooking and the housework and washing his clothes while he contributed nothing.

She replayed in her mind the words that had beguiled her into their hasty marriage. Quite suddenly it occurred to her that he had never once said he loved her. Why then, had he wanted to marry her? Lurking on the edge of her mind was the answer that she could not admit to herself. Simply, it was the only way he could get her to sleep with him.

Then, one morning with Monte lying contentedly in Joe's arms he said, "You're more like a man than a woman, Monte. I've never been with a whore who could please a man like you do, much less one that hungered for it like you do. I always dreamed about a sweet innocent girl I'd have to teach. Somehow, it goes against the grain...."

Her body stiffened in his embrace and she pulled herself upright and climbed out of bed. "You bastard," she grated.

"The women I know don't talk like farmhands," he said coldly.

Monte was shaking with rage. "You ignorant clod, you don't have the slightest idea what a real woman is like. How could you when you were raised by three old maids."

"Don't you even mention my sisters, you're not fit to breathe the same air they do. How could I face them if I brought someone like you home?"

"I don't know, and I don't care. I'm sick of you and your airs about how much better they are than me. My family came from English nobility and my father was educated at Oxford University, so you'll excuse me if I don't get excited about your educated sisters.' At least I've lived. All they've done is sit on the side line and watch life go by while they raised a spoiled selfish ingrate like you.

"The things that happened in my life changed me, and there is no way I can become an innocent virgin again, and I wouldn't if I could. I'm tired of you ordering me around, and trying to make me feel like dirt. I want you to pick up your gear and move out. Get a divorce if you want to, but leave me alone."

"This is easier than I expected," he said insultingly. "I'll take your advice, Madam, and thanks for the parties, it would have cost me more in a whorehouse."

The neighbors had planned a party for the newlyweds and Monte just barely got the news out about the separation in time to stop the celebration. When Sadie brought the two children home expecting to stay for the party she was dumbfounded.

"I really thought things had finally worked out for you," she said, taking Monte in her arms. "Maybe it can be patched up."

A dry-eyed Monte shook her head and finally put into words what deep down she had known all along. "He planned it this way, he had no intention of taking me to his home, and he hated mine. When a woman is fool enough to marry a man who think he's better than her, she's asking for the trouble she'll get. Maybe if I'd let him lord it over me and kowtowed to his every whim.... No, that wouldn't have worked, he'd have lost what little respect he did have for me. It's no use Sadie. It's over." Sadie stayed a few days with Monte who went about her work silently, with no tears, no apparent anger, just a quiet acceptance.

Joe filed for divorce and Monte signed the papers. She had built a wall around her emotions, and wouldn't allow herself the luxury of looking back.

About four months later just as she was putting loaves of bread into the oven to bake, she heard the kitchen door open and turned around. Joe McCune stood in the doorway his black curls glinting in the sunlight that streamed through the door. It was late in February and there were still patches of snow on the ground, but the land was waking up from the long cold winter.

"Monte," he said simply, "I'm sorry. I was wrong about a lot of things. I know now that I love you and I'm willing to give it another try if you are."

The feeling that flooded through her was so exquisite that it was almost pain. She couldn't find her voice so she simply walked into his arms. The children were in school, the smell of fresh baking bread permeated the little house and sunshine beamed through the windows so long

darkened by the gloomy weather. It was a perfect time for regenerating a smoldering passion.

An hour or so later as

they lay in each other's arms they heard a noise at the bedroom door and looked up in time to get a glimpse of Monte's Indian friend as he made a hasty exit and a moment later they heard rapid hoof beats retreating up the road.

Monte would never forget the look on Joe's face or the words said so quietly as be almost inaudible. "You slut, you whoring bitch!" And then he slapped her so hard that she fell back on the bed. She watched in silence as he dressed. She opened her mouth several times to try to explain, but no words would come. She kept wanting to say, "Indians don't knock on doors." Then, suddenly she started to laugh hysterically, the whole thing was so ludicrous, so ridiculous, so unbelievable. Joe gave her a look filled with utter contempt and left. When she stopped laughing she started to sob, her body shook with the violence of her grief.

In the days that followed she was numb with despair. She considered writing Joe a letter to explain that the Indian was only looking for her, intent on getting a loaf of fresh bread, but she knew—with certainty—that he would never believe her. A deep anger began to burn within her. That Joe would believe she could take that old half naked Indian into her bed was almost unendurable. But there was no use in railing at an evil fate, no use to feel sorry for herself. What was done was done, and all Monte could do was to pick up the pieces of her life and go on. The light that had made her such a vibrant person sputtered out.

CHAPTER 10

Several weeks later Monte discovered she was pregnant. She had endured so much that somehow this new development was anti-climactic and she simply accepted it. She no longer projected herself eagerly into the future. Her life had suddenly become threatening. She no longer thought herself capable of handling any difficult situation that faced her. It was a man's world. It was twice as hard for a woman to eke out any kind of living on her own, and her only means of support was taking in laundry or serving in someone else's home. Joe had come into her life and broken her heart and now she was alone again with another child on the way whom she must somehow provide for. She looked ahead to a grim future with no possibility of change.

She had wanted so desperately to make a life for herself and her daughters, to be independent and to be beholden to no man. In any of her relationships with men, she had come out the loser. Why, she wondered must a woman deny her passion, while men were allowed free rein of theirs? When she had surrendered to John Harper at age 17 she became pregnant and suffered the disgrace. Was she so wicked that God intended to punish her for the rest of her life? Was she different from other women? Did other women accept the attentions of their husbands because they were obligated to do so? Was it supposed to be part of the penalty that was exacted of Eve? If so, why did she respond with such joy and abandon?

Loving a man was a dangerous thing to do, and she vowed that it should never happen again. She didn't love Al and their life together had been pleasant. He was a steady worker. Each had done their share, and they had lived comfortably. Their lovemaking had been lacking in ardor, but she had been faithful. He was good to little Ruth and adored their two children, Susie and their son. Alfred became her passion, her dream of the future and had filled in the gap of a loveless marriage.

Could it be that her first sin had been so terrible that part of her penalty was the loss of her son? Who, she thought rebelliously was hurt besides herself? Didn't being a good mother, kind to one's parents and a good wife count for anything? She had always gone to church, and listened to her pastor's teachings, but there was something wrong, something she didn't understand. Why were women judged by such harsh and different standards?

The terrible pain of the loss of her beloved son, and the loss of her security were staggering, but she had buried her losses in hard work and the dream of building security for herself and her two daughters. She was getting along fine all by herself and then Joe had come into her life. Once again, she was alone and again she was forced to face a pregnancy alone. Joe was legally responsible for her child, since the divorce had not become final. She knew she could force him to support her baby, but she recoiled at the thought of a bitter court battle and the charges he would level against her.

Over and over she pondered her dilemma, and finally she decided that being sorry for herself and railing at fate would not solve anything. She could not accept the indignity or the humiliation of trying to make Joe accept his responsibility. If she could only get through the birth of her child she would simply try to survive as she had before Joe entered her life. She would find some way to earn a little cash to supply the necessities that her farm couldn't furnish.

It was late in the spring when she finally wrote to her mother and Lew. In concise unemotional words, she told them all that had happened, even including the part about the Indian. She told them that facing the coming winter alone with a baby due to arrive in November was almost more than she could bear. She wondered if Lew could find it in his heart to help her through this difficult time.

Lew had no trouble making up his mind. Monte needed him. Grover, who was then twenty-three, wanted to accompany Lew to Washington. So, Lew, Grover and Willy boarded a train and arrived in The Dalles in early June, less than a month after Monte's letter had arrived.

Lew and Grover were at work in the sawmill at Klickitat a week after they arrived. They hiked down the slippery hillside covered with fir needles, cutting through the brush as they went along. It was only a three-mile descent to the river below that ran along by the sawmill. After working all day, they climbed back up the steep hill with needed groceries packed on their backs.

The noise of their approach aroused startled deer from their sleep in the thickets and they crashed through the underbrush in fright. Grouse fluttered in awkward flight, making a great commotion, and rabbits darted in zig zag patterns across the trail. It was not uncommon to jump back in alarm as they heard the warning buzz of a timber rattler. It was all new and exciting to the two young men who were raised in a town that was rapidly expanding into a city. They had both worked hard all their lives and were strong and fit so their muscles quickly met the needs of their extra exertions.

The rains started early that fall which shut down logging operations and then, of course, the mill. The two young men worked out in the downpour framing a barn for

Monte and putting a roof over it. With the roof in place they were able to put the siding on and then work on the inside in relative comfort. Before the snow fell they had finished the barn and built a tack room inside which they decided to use for a bedroom. With a small wood stove they managed to live in more comfort than they had in the cramped house where they had been rotating between sleeping on the day bed and the floor.

Lew could scarcely believe that the sister he had been so close to all his life could have changed in just a few short years into the suspicious demanding person she had now become. He told himself that she'd had enough grief to make anyone bitter, but he had a great feeling of loss. He knew with certainty that the warm loyal girl who had been his champion in their youth was gone. She resented the fact that instead of turning their checks over to her the two brothers spent the money on the current bills and materials to build the barn and make improvements on her house. What was left they kept for themselves. Far from appreciating all they were doing for her, she suspected them of conspiring to get her homestead away from her. The arrival of the baby boy on

November 5, 1908, was a pleasant interlude for them
all. Lew had acted as midwife in the uncomplicated
and swift delivery.

The baby was a beautiful child with bright black
curls, large gray eyes and a florid complexion. Monte
to the surprise of them all named him Joe.

"Why didn't you just name him Shit Ass?" demanded
his outraged sister Ruth. She was fourteen and the
embarrassment of her mother having a baby without a
husband was bitter.

They managed to alleviate the boredom through the
cold winter days by playing cards, and listening to Monte
read from the books they had on hand. However, the close
confinement was hard on tempers, and especially for Monte
who was always irritable and hard to please.

At Christmas time Lew saved Monte's house from
utter disaster when the Christmas tree covered with lighted
candles ignited. He snatched a blanket from the couch and
smothered the flames enough so that he could get the tree
out of the house.

Monte found a new complaint to harp on. Ignoring
the fact that her brother's quick action, which could have
resulted in severe burns for him, had saved her house, she
chose to take offense because he had ruined her best
blanket which was burned in so many places that it was no
longer usable. At first Lew let her rave on and then, slow to
anger as he was, he had had enough. That afternoon Lew
mushed out on snowshoes dragging a small sled with Willy
and what few belonging he possessed to the nearest ranch
where they stayed all night and were taken by sled to The
Dalles ferry the next morning.

If Monte had any regrets about her treatment of her
brother she never showed it. She was free of the nagging

fear that he was trying to take her homestead away from her. Grover continued to stay with the family, but Monte could not get along peaceably with anyone. Grover went to work at the mill again in the spring and Monte expected him to hand over his full pay check which Grover did for over a year and then he rebelled. Ruth went to The Dalles and did housework for a family while she went to high school. Monte was frankly glad to get rid of her. She had never been able to get along with Ruth and their mutual love was eroding into something very like hate.

Grover stayed on because he didn't know how Monte could make it on her own and he loved her children. Finally, her temper became too much for even gentle easygoing Grover to bear. He left to join Lew in Portland. Monte was alone with her two-year-old son and nine-yearold   Susie.

CHAPTER 11

Lew was thirty-two when he and Monte had their falling out, and he was scarcely out of sight of the homestead when his anger vanished and was replaced by a heady feeling of euphoria. It was as though a heavy mantle he had carried all his life suddenly slipped from his shoulders.

The only two people in the world he had to worry about was himself and Willy. Grover, by the very act of staying on with Monte, had assumed the responsibility for her and her children. Lew was free!

He had a little money put by, and he had no intention of going back east. He loved all that he had seen so far of the West and had made up his mind to try his fortunes in Portland, Oregon. Lew had no worries about his ability to make a living. He was a good carpenter, a musician, could run a farm and had run a steamroller on paving projects back east. He thought the latter was his best bet in the growing city of Portland where, he had been told, country roads were being changed into paved streets.

He marveled at the magnificent scenery as the train chugged along beside the wide expanse of the Columbia River. The Columbia was so deep that the Indians claimed there were huge sturgeon weighing thousands of pounds lurking in its depths. While Lew took the stories with a grain of salt, it was a fascinating possibility. Steep hills smothered with timber climbed into the sky on both the Washington and Oregon sides of the river, and snowcapped mountains loomed in the distance. The train huffed and puffed to a stop at Multnomah Falls and all the passengers from the East got out for a few minutes to gaze in wonder at the majestic avalanche of water that tumbled from the rocks far up on a hillside. Willy clung tightly to his father and hid his head against Lew's sleeve frightened at the enormity of the waterfall.

The train arrived in Portland late in the afternoon and as they were standing at the station a little black boy about Willy's age came up to them and stood staring up at Lew's height. "Man, oh man! Will you look at that walking 'telefoam' pole!" he exclaimed. Lew joined in the general laughter that followed.

Lew found his way about Portland rapidly and he and Willy lived in a boarding house for the first six months, and then Lew who was an accomplished poker player got into a big game at a gambling house. It was one of those nights when the cards kept coming his way, and when he was able to pocket $300, which was a good amount in those days, he decided to quit. His decision was not exactly met with approval. Lew wasn't happy with being called an

eastern sharpie who dropped in and ran off as soon as he won a pot. "All right," he said, "I'll play until I lose what I have in front of me or until I win a thousand dollars." He knew that two of the fellows were playing together, out to get him and he suspected them of trying to run him out of the pot by raising on bad hands.

It was getting late and Lew decided he would play only one more hand. It was five-card draw and he was pleased when he picked up three deuces. The betting was lively and Lew suspected that his three deuces were not going to hold up. He considered folding when he got a funny hunch that he should stay. The big fellow on his right bet fifty dollars, Lew called. One of the players dropped, two more stayed and then the one whom Lew suspected of being in cahoots with the original bettor, raised. It was too late to get out then, so Lew called and raised. Everyone dropped out except Lew and the two professionals. Lew made a silent promise that, win or lose he would never seriously gamble again. One of the fellows drew three cards and the other one drew one. Lew drew two. Slowly he squeezed his cards, the first one was a ten, and the next one was a deuce! His face was impassive as he tossed two hundred dollars on the table.

There was a moment of dead silence, one of the men gave Lew a hard-penetrating gaze and threw in his cards. Now it was time for the opposition to do some considering. The original bettor called and raised another two hundred. Lew knew that fellow was not a fool, so the guy must have a good hand. Lew figured that he could be betting on a high full house, or even four of a kind. Maybe even a royal flush. Well, Lew could beat the full and you didn't get four of a kind every day even if it was four little deuces, so it was worth a call.

Lew called and held his breath. The other gambler fanned out his cards on the table. Three aces and two kings.

"That' a good hand," Lew said softly, as he laid out his hand four deuces and his ten," but not good enough."

He left the saloon with over a thousand dollars in his pocket. The next day he bought a two-story house on Grand Avenue with a bathroom that boasted a real bathtub. There was enough money left to furnish it. Lew and Willy had their own home! He kept his promise about never gambling seriously again. Superstition or not he felt that some presence had helped him and he would honor his promise.

Lew hired a series of house keepers in the next several years. Some left because of unwanted advances from him and some left rebuffed, when they became too possessive. A little red headed pepper pot, named Belle, stayed the longest. She fell in love with Lew immediately, and wanted their relationship to be permanent, but knowing how shy Lew was of serious entanglements, she wisely put no pressure on him. Then, of course, he was still married and a divorce was almost impossible to obtain in Illinois when one spouse was mentally ill. Lew was so fond of Belle that finally he gently broke off their relationship. He didn't want to hurt her and he thought she deserved a husband and the chance to raise a family. To his surprise, she almost immediately married another man. Finding a housekeeper who was not interested in marriage and one whom he found attractive was not easy. He was young and virile and wanted to make love to them with no strings attached. He always said that the ones he wanted didn't want him, and the ones who wanted him he didn't want.

The next two years he spent in Portland were the most carefree of his life. He had his share of lady friends, he made good money and Willy was healthy and a good student. Lew liked running the big steamroller that smoothed out the paving on the streets and he played guitar or violin with a dance band so he was busy and seldom bored with his life. But there was something missing, and sometimes he found himself thinking about Laura and wondering if she was happy. Looking back from a more mature standpoint, he knew he would not have married Elsie and thereby changed the whole pattern of his life if he'd been older and a little wiser. He had always wanted a home and lots of children, and it seemed he was fated to be always on the outside looking in.

He met Faye and Otto Davis at a dance where he was playing. They took an instant liking to the handsome young man. They invited him to their house for supper one night. They had decided to do a little matchmaking and had invited Faye's sister, Bessie, too.

Lew fell head over heels in love with the tiny doll like Bessie. Somehow, he found himself comparing her with Laura. She had the same sweet gentle way about her. When he found out that she had a little daughter to support he was delighted, he wanted nothing more than to take care of Bessie and her little girl.

The first thing he did as he mounted his campaign to win Bessie was to hire an attorney to try to get a divorce from Elsie. Then he fired his housekeeper and entreated Bessie to come and keep house for him. She needed the money and jobs were hard for women to find in those days except as domestic help in another woman's home. Bessie thought she could handle Lew and it would be nice to be in charge of a house for the first time in her life. Lew and Bessie's life together was very much like any other young couple in their day except that Bessie and Doris shared a room, and Lew was so in love with her that he was able to abide by her rules. Faye and Otto visited them often and Bessie turned out to be a neat housekeeper and a good cook. All would have been well except that Willy and Doris were both badly spoiled and neither Bessie nor Lew approved of the other's child rearing methods.

Eleven-year-old Willy deeply resented Bessie and made her life miserable when his father wasn't home. He was sassy and rude and refused to accept any kind of discipline from her. When his father was home he was a model child, so that Lew didn't quite realize what a problem he was.

Doris was two years old and a little terror. When things didn't go her way, she would lie down on the floor and kick and scream. Lew worried for fear the neighbors would think he was beating her. The two children were bent on wrecking any kind of peace that might have prevailed. One night when he came home he found that Bessie had packed her bags and left.

Lew was devastated. His first impulse was to run after her and bring her back, but if there was one thing he had learned, it was the folly of trying to live in a home upset by strife. After all, even if she had returned his love, which he knew she did not, what could he offer her? He couldn't marry her until his divorce was granted, and who knew when that would be? No, he would let her go.

Willy had been invited to go up to the mountains with a friend and his family, and Lew could hardly bear to go home to the desolate house. One evening as he walked along the street on his way home he was so overwhelmed with grief that he thought he could not bear to enter his empty home. He had worked late and a light rain was falling. The streets were empty but lights glowed from the windows, as he passed by, making prisms in the water gleaming in the street. All Lew had ever wanted was a home, a loving wife and lots of children and it seemed that he was to be forever denied.

As he walked up his front steps, he realized that a light was glowing from the front window. His heart began to beat wildly, Bessie had come back! As he opened the door a rush of warmth and the heavenly fragrance of cooking stew greeted him. Then out of the kitchen with a colorful apron tied around her waist came red headed Belle. Lew tried unsuccessfully to hide his disappointment. Belle had been his housekeeper when he met Bessie. He had broken up with her with   some reluctance as well as guilt. Their relationship had been intimate and she wanted a commitment from him.

Belle laughed, "Come on now, Lew, I'm not that little black headed witch, but aren't you glad to see me?"

Suddenly Lew was delighted, he'd always liked Belle and they'd had great fun together. This certainly beat coming home to a cold house. He gathered her in a big bear hug.

After dinner Belle went upstairs and came down with a baby in her arms. "This is Jenny," she told Lew.

The little blonde, blue eyed girl appeared to be about six months old. He looked at Belle questioningly.

"I know what you're thinking, Lew, and you're right. She could be your baby and I'll be honest with you, I'm not sure myself. Jim Fessler married me right off after I left here. He never had any doubts but that she was his child, so that's the way it is."

"Where is he now?" Lew asked.

"He's dead," said Belle flatly. "He was killed on the railroad and he left a little pension for Jenny and me, so don't think I came here for charity. I still love you, Lew. I always have. When I found out Miss high falutin' Bessie had left you, I thought you might appreciate someone who loves you."

Lew let Belle and Jenny stay with some misgivings. He liked Belle, but there was an ache in his chest for Bessie and it wouldn't go away. He didn't want to lead Belle on so he told her how he felt.

"Don't worry," she said cheerfully. "I'll stay here and take care of you and Willy as long as you need me. If things don't turn out, well, they don't turn out. In the meantime, we need each other."

Lew loved the baby, and he often thought how sensible it would be to marry Belle when he was free. They'd probably have a house full of the kids that had always been his dream, but there was a certain crudeness about Belle that disturbed him. She was loud talking and her grammar jolted his sensibilities. She lacked the class of both Laura and Bessie. Somehow, he couldn't imagine being married to her.

One evening as he came off work, he looked up to see Bessie sitting in a little buggy waiting for him. He tried to control the emotions that overwhelmed him. He felt giddy, his heart pounded against his ribs and his breath was short as he approached the carriage.

"Well, hello," he said with as much calm as he could muster.

There was a mischievous twinkle in her eye, as she took his hand. "I gottum, I no wantum, I no gotum I wantum." she said. Then in a more serious tone, "Lew, I want to come back to you. I didn't realize how I felt about you. One of my mother's boarders, George Stange, has taken a shine to me and Mama thinks I should marry him. When I compare him with you, I know I could never be happy with him."

"He can marry you, I can't," said Lew turning away so she could not see the hurt in his eyes.

"I don't care, Lew. We both want the same kind of life, and that's important. George Stange is a stableman, and that is all he'll ever be. I don't want the kind of life I'd have with him." She was pleading, "I know I've been a fool, Chauncey has stood between me and my ability to love anyone else. It's a kind of insanity. I think I've been trying to get even with you for the way Chauncey treated me. Can you understand that?"

"Not really," said Lew honestly. "I don't feel that I deserve being second best, but I do understand what you mean by a 'kind of insanity' it's what overcomes me when I see you. But, Bessie, I don't think that's enough to make a marriage work, and even if it is, I can't marry you until my divorce goes through, and I have no guarantee that it will ever be granted. The way I feel about you, I want to live with you as man and wife and I can't do that, either. What if I should get you in the family way? No, Bessie, I think we'd better leave well enough alone. I don't think you really love me, and it takes a lot of love to make a marriage work. You know that Belle has come back?"

Bessie nodded her head. "I know, and I'd be making the biggest mistake of my life if I let her have you. I wish we could get married, and I know you're doing everything you can to make that possible. I've thought it all over, and I'm willing to live with you as your wife. As for me getting in the family way, you don't have to worry about that. When Doris was born I was badly injured and the doctor said I wouldn't ever have any more babies."

Lew was surprised at the feeling of loss that came over him. He loved Bessie and he wanted her, but he wanted more children. If he married Belle he would raise her little girl as his own (there was always the possibility that she was his) and they could have other children.

He could not get over the feeling that Bessie didn't love him as he loved her. He suspected that she was more motivated by the security he could offer her than by love. He felt strongly that Molly was pressuring Bessie to marry George, and that Bessie was turning to him as the lesser of two evils. He had met George Stange at Molly's house on one occasion and had thought him something of a clod. The thought of Bessie marrying George was unthinkable.

Suddenly his heart melted. How could he ever live without her? He swung her out of the buggy and into his arms. As he kissed her tear wet face, Lew made his decision. Bessie must, at least, love him a little if she was willing to come back to him.

Grover had moved away from Monte, and bought a little truck farm in Mosier, Oregon. He was visiting Lew when Lew returned home that night after his conversation with Bessie. Lew was trying to find some way to approach the subject of his reconciliation with Bessie. He couldn't think of any way to tell Belle without hurting her.

They were sitting at the table with Grover and Belle talking while Lew sat in uneasy silence. Belle looked at him keenly.

"What's on your mind, Lew?" she asked.

Lew felt the blood rise in his face.

"Lew, you made up with her, didn't you?"

Lew was so surprised that all he could mumble was, "How did you know?"

"As transparent as you are, Lew, how could I not know?" Belle was shaken. She knew intuitively that she had lost him. Then she burst out, "You're a fool Lew, that little black headed devil will bring you nothing but trouble. Don't you know that?"

Grover, who had been witnessing the little drama, suddenly jumped into the void.

"Belle," he said eagerly, "I need someone to keep house for me, I have a nice little farm and a job on the railroad. We can get married. I fell for you the minute I saw you. I know this isn't a very romantic proposal, but if you'll take me up on it, you'll never be sorry. Why don't you come home with me? You know I'll be good to little Jenny and I'll take care of you for as long as we live." Two weeks later they were married. (note: Belle subsequently bore Grover six children and they lived out their lives together).

CHAPTER 12

Many times, Lew asked himself, "Should a man marry the woman he loves or the woman who loves him?" Except for Willy's obvious disapproval and Doris's temper tantrums, Lew and Bessie settled into a life very much like any married couple. Bessie was happy in what she had come to think of as her home. She had a knack for making a house beautiful.   There were always bowls of flowers or arrangements of some kind of greenery when the flowers were gone. The furniture was tastefully arranged with little accents artfully set about. Molly and Fay were frequent visitors and Bessie could almost forget that she was not Lew's legal wife. The attorney kept telling them that things were working out and it wouldn't be too long until the divorce was granted. All they could do, he said, was wait and try to be patient.

Despite their unconventional arrangement they could have been happy except for Willy's obvious disapproval and Bessie's inability to control her spoiled and willful child who threw temper tantrums at the slightest obstruction of her wishes. Lew tried his best to be a father to the little girl and she was so sweet when she wanted to be that he was sure she'd straighten up in time and he began to love her.

Willy was still a handful and resented the intrusion of Bessie and Doris into a life where once he had had his father all to himself.

Bessie didn't like Willy any more than he liked her, and nothing Lew could do would change things.

One afternoon Bessie and Lew took Doris down to the shoe store to get a pair of much needed shoes. Because

rain was so prevalent in Portland they bought the child a pair of high topped shoes. Doris didn't say a word as they were buttoned onto her little feet, but they   were no   more than out of the store until she threw herself on the side walk and began kicking the toes of her shoes against the cement and screaming. "I hate these shoes, I won't these shoes, I won't wear them." Heads were turning at the   racket, and   the owner of the shoe store came out to see what the ruckus was about. Bessie was trying to placate the youngster.

"It's all right, baby, you don't have to wear them if you don't want to," she soothed.

Doris was ruining the shoes so they couldn't be returned and suddenly Lew lost his patience. He picked up the surprised child and swatted her across the bottom with a resounding whack. She stopped screaming as though she'd been turned off. Bessie grabbed Doris in her arms. "How dare you lay a hand on my child?" she grated, "I promise you, you'll never get to do it again. Why don't you beat up on that big oaf of a son of yours instead of picking on a three-year old baby?

They walked home in silence and the only words Lew uttered as she stood at the door with her packed suitcases were, "This is your decision, Bessie, remember that, and once you go through that door we are through."

"Don't worry, Lew Hibberd. "I've had all I can take of you and that -that insolent son of yours. I thought I could learn to love you, but it's no use. Maybe you can find some other woman with a child you can beat."

Bessie's attack was so unfair, that Lew didn't even bother to answer. She had never loved him, he thought bitterly, and he'd been a fool living in a fool's paradise. He carried her bags to the street car and helped Bessie and Doris onto the car. Then he went home and looked around the silent house. He squared his shoulders and promised himself that he would never look back. It was over and done with and he would start a new life.

The next day he packed everything that was Bessie's into boxes. As was always the case with Lew when there was a serious problem, he was offered a job helping to build the highway along the Columbia River from The Dalles to Portland. He accepted the job. He decided to board up the house until he could decide what to do with it. Willy could stay in Mosier with Belle and Grover.

As he was finishing up his work and getting ready to cover the windows his next-door neighbor, whom he had known since he first bought the house, opened the front door and called, "Lew".

"Lew, I don't mean to interfere. But it looks like you and Bessie have parted company again and you are about to close up your house."

Without giving him a chance to reply, she rattled on. "My sister and her family are here from New York and they need a house, her husband's been transferred out here. Would you be willing to rent it to them for a few months until they find a place to buy? She's a wonderful housekeeper and you could just leave everything as is."

,

CHAPTER 13

Bessie hadn't stopped to think how her mother would feel when she came back home again. Molly was furious. She had married Lawrence Hall and for the first time in her life was free of debts and the necessity of making a living. She and Lawrence enjoyed each other's company and had fun together. He disapproved of Doris heartily and the way Bessie was raising her. Having them in the house would cause nothing but trouble.

"You make your bed, Bessie, and you want me to lie in it," Molly said bitterly. "Lew didn't hurt your precious child, what she needs is a little discipline. You threw away your chance for a good home with a man who loves you. Do you think any other man will put up with that child? It's not her fault she's like she is, it's yours. Everything isn't going to happen just like you want it to, Miss Bessie, and you can just go right back to Lew where you belong."

Bessie started to cry, "Mama, please. Lew won't take me back, he already told me that."

"All right Bessie, you can stay here for a few days and consider it a visit. By that time Lew will have calmed down and I'll take you back to him."

Bessie looked into her mother's face, and she knew she had no recourse, but to do as she was told. Suddenly she was terrified! She had burned her bridges. Lew would never take her back. He'd know Molly had forced her to go back, and Lew was too proud to take her on those terms. What was to become of her and her little girl?

Bessie cried herself sick for the next couple of days. In that time, she asked herself over and over, what had come over her to make her fly off the handle as she had. She knew she'd been unfair to Lew, and she knew that she did care for him.

Bessie's tears had no effect on an implacable Molly and she offered not a word of consolation. Four days after Bessie left Lew, Molly loaded her and her things into a light buggy and drove her back to Lew's house. When they drove up in front there were children playing on the sidewalk. Molly and Bessie walked up to the door and rang the doorbell which was answered by a pleasant young woman. A shocked Molly asked for Lew. The young woman told them she had leased the house fully furnished from Mr. Hibberd. She was bubbling, "We just arrived from New York and I can't believe we were so lucky. Imagine! Finding a house so beautifully furnished so fast. It will give us plenty of time to find a house of our own."

Bessie thought for a moment that she would be sick, she swayed against her mother and would have fallen.

"Did Mr. Hibberd say where he was going?" Molly asked.

"No, he said he'd be out of town and he'd let us know when he got settled.

Bessie was numbed with despair. The drive back to her mother's house seemed endless.

"I don't know why, Bessie, but you seem to have a talent for ruining your life and expecting other people to rescue you. I've been thinking on it and you're just going to have to marry George Stange. He's wanted you for years, he's a good hard-working man and he'll provide for you as best he can."

"But Mama, he's only a stableman. What kind of a life will I have? And I don't love him."

"Love!" said Molly coldly. "You loved Chauncey Miller and what did that get you? You won't have the kind of life you would have had with Lew, but at least you'll eat regularly. You know, Bessie, not many men are going to want to marry you. Men want virgins, and they don't want to raise some other man's child. You don't have a lot of choice, do you?"

Bessie couldn't believe her mother. How could she turn against her own daughter? Even as Bessie asked herself that desperate question, she knew that Molly loved her and thought that this was the best solution for all of them.

As they drew up in front of Molly's house, she turned to Bessie. "I know you think I'm hard, Bessie, but there is no other way. I don't have to tell you that I've worked hard all my life and I can't afford to lose what I've finally got. Lawrence likes you, but you've spoiled Doris so bad that there isn't any way she's going to fit into a household without causing a lot of trouble. It just wouldn't be fair to Lawrence. I don't want to be mean, but two extra mouths to feed makes the difference between things being easy for Lawrence and not having to scrimp and scrape again.

"George is crazy in love with you, and you won't be the first woman who learned to love a man after she married him. I don't know what possessed you to throw away the kind of life you would have had with Lew."

"I don't know either, Ma." Bessie's voice was almost inaudible. "I'll do whatever you think best, but just give me a few days to think about it."

"No," said Molly firmly, "the more you think and stew about it the harder it will be. I'm going to invite George over tomorrow night and I'll talk to him, the rest is up to you."

Bessie tossed and turned the whole night through, her head ached and her stomach felt queasy. There was no other way out, but to marry George. At least she'd be a respectable woman for the first time. She thought of Lew and she was filled with regret. Why had she so stubbornly refused to love him? Why hadn't she made more of an effort to win Willy over? She knew in her heart that Lew loved little Doris, and wanted to be a father to her. She could not understand why she couldn't bear to have anyone even say a cross word to Doris.

She went to the window and looked out at the star strewn night, the trees were still baring from the winter and their branches made strange patterns in the darkness. Somewhere in the distance she heard a rooster crow. She thought of Lew and how he always got up in the early morning, washed his hands and then went down to build a fire in the kitchen stove. She remembered regretfully how she had teased him and said he should build the fire first and then wash. Lew was always so scrupulously clean about his person, and so particular about his clothes.

A stab of pain seemed to pierce her heart. It was her fault that she had lost him, but then if he'd really loved her, why didn't he wait just a little longer before he made everything so final? He had told her about Elsie and the hell he had lived through, and suddenly she understood. Lew was as scarred as she was. He was afraid to risk another unhappy alliance, and she had given him little assurance that they could have a happy home.

Suddenly George crowded into her thoughts and she could see him with his sandy hair, his pale, water blue eyes and the wad of tobacco that bulged from his cheek. She heard the nasal twang of his voice and saw the dirt lined nails of his work callused hands. He always looked rumpled and in need of a haircut and shave. God help her. What had she done? No, she decided, she could not marry George. Somehow, she'd find work, maybe Faye and Otto would let her stay with them until she got on her feet.

But how could she stand up to her mother? She wished she was strong like Fay, or had Ina's quiet determination. She and Jasper had no fight in them, it was almost as though they didn't belong to the rest of the family. As dawn began to filter through the curtains she crawled shivering into bed and fell asleep, but when Doris awakened her an hour or two later the problem was still there.

That night she sat in the parlor with George, her mother and Lawrence, and listened to them talk. Her eyes kept closing. She felt someone take her hand and opened her eyes to see George smiling adoringly down at her.

"Poor little Bessie," he said gently. "You're really tired."

The unexpected sympathy almost undid Bessie and she came closer to caring about him in that minute than she ever would again. It was good to have someone who would look after her. Her last thought as she went to sleep that night was that she wasn't strong enough to fight them all and she'd have to marry George and make the best of it. Several days later they set the date for the wedding. Bessie insisted on waiting a month to give her some time to get ready, and the date was set for early March which gave her a month and the forlorn hope that Lew would come back to her.

She had been suffering from nausea for several weeks, but she didn't think too much about it because of her mental state. Then one morning it occurred to her that it had been almost two months since her last 'sick time'. The doctor had told her that she wouldn't ever be able to get in the family way again, or had he said she wasn't likely to? The thought that she might be carrying Lew's child was so shocking that her mind could scarcely grasp it. She waited another week, and her suspicions became reality. She was in the family way, and she had no idea how to resolve this new problem.

She'd written several letters to Lew asking them to be forwarded. All of them came back with "address unknown" stamped on them. Where had he gone?

The days marched inexorably on with her wedding day getting closer and closer. What if she just married George and didn't tell anyone? What could he do when he found out? Even as the thought crossed her mind she rejected it. Finally, she was driven to telling Molly. She would never forget the look on her mother's face as she finally blurted out her dilemma, and how her mother groped for the nearest chair and literally fell into it.

"What are we going to do now?" Molly's question was almost a groan. She sat silently, thinking, and Bessie stared out the window blindly, unable to look at her mother.

"Well," she said finally, "George won't be happy with this new development, but I think he wants you badly enough to marry you anyway."

Bessie listened, heartsick, as her mother almost bargained with George. He was no longer the eager suitor putting his best foot forward to win her, and she could no longer treat him with the kind of condescension that had thinly veiled her reluctance to marry him. She prayed silently that he would refuse to marry her. Somehow, she'd find Lew. She remembered his disappointment when she told him that they could never have a child. She also knew that if George agreed to marry her she could never go against her determined mother. She wrote one last desperate letter to Lew which didn't come back.

"I'll marry her, just like we planned," said George magnanimously, "and the child can have my name, but after that I won't have no more to do with it. You'll have to find a family to adopt it. I don't think it's fair to ask me to bring up two young'uns that ain't mine. Dorse is a real handful and that's about all I can rightly be asked to take on."

Bessie winced. Why couldn't he say Doris? It was always Dorse. She looked pleadingly at her mother, numb with despair. Molly's face was hard and relentless. She was determined that Bessie should not bear another child out of wedlock.

"We'll try to find Lew and give him first chance to take his child, if not we'll find a good home for it."

"But Ma, I can't just give my own baby away like it was a puppy or a kitten." Bessie protested, her eyes bright with tears. What would people say?"

"People have their own problems," said Molly coldly. "As far as anybody will know or care you could have lost the child stillborn. It won't be easy, Bessie, but you and George will have children of your own. If we can find Lew, he'll take the baby and he'll give it a good life, too."

Molly hardened her heart against the stricken look on Bessie's face. "Now you listen to me, Bessie, you keep getting yourself in these messes, and now you have a chance to turn your life around and be a respected woman. There's no use in crying over spilt milk. What's done is done and you should be grateful to have a good man like George to stand by you."

George who had been listening quietly was angry, he should just leave Miss Bessie to stew in her own juice. She obviously didn't appreciate what he was doing for her. Even as the thoughts flitted through his mind, he knew that he'd never let Bessie go, but one thing he wouldn't do was raise another child fathered by a man who had been Bessie's lover.

Early in March Bessie Hughes promised to love, honor and obey George Stange until death did them part. She resolved to make the best of things and tried to wall up all the dreams and plans she'd once had. She had pledged herself to a station in life from which she could never escape. The only thing she could do was to try to see that Doris had a better chance. She made a valiant effort to discipline the little girl so that George would have less to complain about. He disliked the child, she knew that, but he never raised a hand against her. Instead he did little underhanded things to upset her so that he could appeal to Bessie. She sometimes felt as though she was living in an armed camp.

The first few months of their marriage was a total disaster. He wanted her to love him because he had rescued her and made her his wife, and he tried to force her to show a little humbleness by reminding her on every occasion what she owed him. He discovered, to his surprise, that inside the soft pliant little Bessie was a woman of pride and she would not bend to him. It didn't help matters for him to wake up at night and reach over to her to find her pillow wet with tears.

George was a good man. He loved Bessie and he wanted her to love him more than anything in the world. When it finally dawned on him that far from winning her love he was making her hate him, he changed his tactics.

One night in halting words he tried to make Bessie understand how he felt. "We've been going at things all wrong," he conceded. "You know how I feel about you and I can't stand for you to be so unhappy. Maybe we could talk things over, you act like you hate me and I don't think I deserve that."

"No, you don't," said Bessie quietly, "but I don't think I deserve to be made to feel constantly beholden to you, either. I didn't ask you to marry me. My mother and you fixed that up between yourselves. You married me for reasons of your own, and I'm not going to be made to feel like a poor relation in my own house. But you're going to have to make some concessions, too.

Things went a little smoother after that, but George couldn't help the deep resentment at the unfairness of his wife's feeling toward him.

He took a lot of his anger out on Doris in the subtlest ways, but somehow, they managed a semblance of domestic harmony.

CHAPTER 14

It was four months after Lew had left Portland before he sent in a change of address for his mail. He thought he had built a wall against further hurt, but when he read the last of the letters from Bessie before she married George his sorrow was so great that the pain in his chest was suffocating. Thank God they wanted him to take the baby. The thought of his child and Bessie's going to some stranger was unthinkable. When he told Grover and Belle he couldn't help but catch the gleam of malice in Belle's eyes, but she was basically a kind person and even though she was in the early months of pregnancy herself she offered to take Lew's baby and raise it with her own. Lew could not but be touched by the gesture, but he thought he could care for his child himself. He owned his own home, and he'd get a housekeeper. His tenants had found a house and they would be moved out by the time he got back to Portland. In the few remaining months, he had a great deal of time to think and regret the haste with which he had let his relationship with Bessie be terminated. He even thought about names for the baby, he decided that if it were a girl he'd name her Mary Laurraine after Molly whose real name was Mary, and after his lost Laura whose name was Laurraine. He couldn't ever decide on a name for a boy.

One night he dreamed that he had gone to pick up his child and when he opened the blanket to look at the little face the blanket was empty. Lew, then fully realized how much he wanted the infant, and began to worry that when it came to the moment of parting that Bessie would not give up her child. He went to visit Molly after he got back to Portland and put his worry into words.

"Bessie's had enough trouble with George over Doris, she knows you will be good to your baby. I sometimes feel very guilty about all this," Molly confessed. "You couldn't marry her anyway, so it seemed the best thing for her to marry George."

Lew turned on Molly, his eyes flashing anger, "You knew I'd take care of her, you could have waited a little while."

"Now look, Lew, if you're going to place any blame, you'd best look in the mirror. Why did you let her come running home every time some little problem came up? I don't know why your children think you are obligated to keep rescuing them no matter how old they get. Can't you understand that I couldn't let Bessie have another child out of wedlock?"

"I don't understand any of it," said Lew sadly, "I don't know if some kind of evil fate hangs over some people or why things happen the way they do. We all share in the blame and all we can do now is try to make the best of it. I'll love and take care of that child, and it will have the best I can give it."

CHAPTER 15

Bessie tried to change her position so as not to awaken her sleeping husband. The heavy humidity was unbearable and her back ached with a vicious grinding agony. There was no way for her to get comfortable, so quietly she eased herself out of bed and padded into the kitchen. The floor boards felt rough—but cool—to her bare feet. The time for the arrival of the baby was little more than a month away. Poor little thing, she tried not to think of it except in a detached sort of way as though she were harboring a strange little life that really didn't belong to her. All the arrangements had been made for Lew to pick up the infant as soon as it was born.

At the thought of Lew her heart squeezed painfully. All the time she had lived with him she hadn't realized how good he was to her. If it hadn't been for Doris and Willy maybe things could have worked out for them. Deep in her heart she knew that the problem hadn't been the children, it was Chauncey that had stood between them. Somehow, she couldn't stop herself from trying to make Lew pay for what Chauncey had done to her. How would Lew manage to care for another child, she wondered?

She went over to the sink and grasping the handle of the pump she began to fill a basin with water. She splashed her face and neck, grateful for the instant relief from the oppressive heat. It must be going to rain she thought, probably one of those sudden Oregon summer storms that split the sky with jagged streaks of light followed by a thunderous cacophony of sound that rolled across the heavens. Bessie shivered, not from fear, but from the strange excitement that always invaded her being when the forces of nature were so awesomely at war.

She walked heavily over to the kitchen table and gingerly pulled out a chair so as not to make any noise. She knew if she awakened George he'd angrily order her back to bed with a lecture about her difficulties in keeping up with the housework and her wifely duties in the best of circumstances. Staying up all hours of the night just made an extra burden on him, he'd say. Bessie so wanted a little time to herself and so seldom got it.

When George was at work there was the never-ending housework, the clothes to be scrubbed, and the big iron cook stove —her mortal enemy— to cope with. It had an insatiable need for more and more wood that had to be brought from the woodshed to the bin in the kitchen. The stove would turn a violent red, burning anything in the oven and boiling over the things on top of the stove, or the fire would sputter and die leaving the bread in the oven a soggy mess never to rise again. Then black smoke would curl out all around the stove lids in swirls that looked like mocking smiles.

And there was always three-year-old Doris clinging to her skirts and demanding her undivided attention. She adored her little daughter, but there was never any time to read or write or do any of the things she wanted to do for herself. The constant struggle to keep peace between the child and George was wearing. She knew Doris was spoiled, which was a combination of her inability to refuse the child anything she could provide for her and the result of having been an only child in a household of adoring adults. Thwarting Doris in any way would bring on an instant tantrum with kicking and screaming and Bessie trying desperately to placate her. George was far from blameless, either. He was jealous of the child and would deliberately bait her. The thought of the scene enacted the day before brought a quick flush of anger to her face. George had been sucking noisily on a piece of hard candy.

"I don't know why your daughter has to hound me all the time, I can't even eat a piece of candy without her trying to get away from me," George whined. "A man can't have any peace in his own house. It ain't as if I didn't already give her three pieces and I think that's enough for any child."

"She's only three years old," said Bessie placatingly, "she doesn't understand why if you're eating candy she can't have some, too."

"Didn't I just tell you that I already gave her some? I can't help it if she chews it all up instead of sucking it and making it last."

Doris started to scream and stamp her feet.
Bessie's eyes filled with tears.

"Now you're going to start bawling," George yelled. Then quietly, "Oh to hell with it, give the damn little bastard her way like you always do. All I'm worth to you is somebody to break my back working so's I can bring the money in, that's all you care about. Here, brat, take it, you want it so bad," and he flung the sack of candy at Doris. They were standing on the porch and Bessie watched with a sick feeling in the pit of her stomach as the sack broke and the hard candies went rolling down the steps bouncing as they went. George turned and stalked back into the house while Doris ran about gleefully gathering up the candy, dirt, leaves and all.

Bessie felt helpless, she was completely unable to control the situation. She knew with sad certainty that another child who was not his would make life unbearable for both her and the children. No matter how she regretted that decision, she knew that she must relinquish her child as soon as it was born. Bessie was caught in a trap from which there was no escape.

She felt old and defeated at twenty-four. Softly she tiptoed onto the front porch and sat on the porch swing, arranging the pillows to try to ease the pain in her back.

She looked up at the star strewn heavens, and thought   how infinitesimal she was in the grand scheme of things.   A bird twittered sleepily in the gnarled old apple tree. Her big gray cat came and jumped up on the swing settling himself comfortably at her side purring so softly that Bessie was forced to smile. Tom was no more eager to awaken George than she was. He hated the cat and Bessie suspected that showing his open dislike for it made up a little bit for being forced to tolerate her child. Why, she wondered, had she so perversely clung to her fruitless love for Chauncey Miller? He had deserted her when she so desperately needed him and brought shame on her and her family. Far too late she realized that her stubborn inability to relinquish that dream had brought her nothing but sorrow.

Almost imperceptibly a soft breeze ruffled the leaves of the trees and slowly, gently, rain drops began to fall. The instant relief from the stifling heat was wonderful and Bessie snuggled down against the pillows trying to get as comfortable as her swollen body would allow. The steady patter of the rain and the purring of the cat were almost hypnotic and slowly her eyes closed.

CHAPTER 16

Her mind was spinning backwards and suddenly Bessie was in the parlor on Elm Street, dusting the window sills when she saw a tall, rather elegant looking man walking up the street. He paused for a moment in front of their house and then turned and came up the steps. The clang of the doorbell reverberated through the house. Bessie straightened her apron and dabbed nervous fingers at the straying tendrils of her hair and then went to the door.

"I'm Chauncey Miller," he said directly, "and if this is the right address, I understand that you have a room to let."

"Yes, we do," said Bessie. "Please come in, I'll call Mama." She asked him to sit on the formal high-backed bench that sat in the hall. She would have liked to seat him in the parlor, but her mother would have disapproved. One didn't invite strangers into one's parlor.

Bessie watched, her heart swelling with pride as her mother came down the stairs. There was an air about Molly. She was a very attractive woman, but it was the regal way she carried herself that gave her scant five feet an illusion of height. There was an air of quality about Molly.

Bessie went back to her work in the parlor and left Molly to talk to Mr. Miller. Her heart was beating a little harder than necessary, and she tried not to let herself think how much she hoped Mr. Miller would take the room. Everything about Chauncey Miller appealed to Bessie. He was cultured, she could tell that by the way he spoke. She thought he was probably in his late thirties and she considered him very handsome in a slender aristocratic way.

For Bessie to be so attracted to a man was unusual. She was almost twenty and had turned down the offer of marriage from several young men. Most of the young men she knew were railroad workers or the sons of farmers and they all seemed impossibly young and boring to her. Bessie had read every book she could get her hands on since she was a child, and despite her lack of formal schooling she was more educated than she realized. She knew the rest of her family thought she was too particular and that she'd probably end up an old maid. Her dream was to go to school and get her teaching credential, but with seven boarders and the big house to keep Bessie was needed at home.

She was overjoyed when her mother came into the parlor a little later and told her that Chauncey Miller would be back as soon as he could have his belongings picked up at the depot and brought to the house. After Bessie had the new boarder's room in order she filled a vase with spring flowers and set it on the bureau.

From the first day Bessie had seen Chauncey coming up the street she had day dreamed about him. His fine thinly chiseled features, even the meticulous way in which he combed his hair so carefully to cover his receding forehead set him apart from the other men who lived at their boarding house. Chauncey worked at the train station as a ticket agent and he was always clean and fresh shaven in contrast to the construction men who were good pay but a loud and bawdy bunch. They spent their evenings playing cards in the dining room after supper, or drinking down at the saloon. Chauncey spent his free time reading, a pastime to which Bessie was also addicted. He was working to get a college education, he told Bessie, and she was enormously impressed. His thirty-eight years didn't present too much of an age difference to Bessie, it just made her more respectful of his opinions and experience.

The relationship between Chauncey and Bessie flowered slowly. At first, they talked of books and poetry, and then their conversations turned to life and love. On Sundays after church Bessie and Chauncey would stroll home from the services deep in conversation, and then their strolls started turning into long walks when the weather permitted.

Molly was a great mimic and sometimes when Bessie and Chauncey were out walking she'd pretend to walk with the cane he affected. Holding her head so that it looked as though she were smelling something odious, and poking his pretended cane about she'd nod to her delighted spectators and say, "Howja do." in a high nasal voice. No one could understand what it was about Chauncey that so fascinated Bessie. Men considered him a puny excuse for a man, and most women considered him stuck up and a dreadful bore totally devoid of personality.

On one of their walks he finally told Bessie how dear she had become to him, and of course Bessie was already head over heels in love. No one had ever read poetry to her before, or deplored the fact that she was born into a station so beneath her. When he first kissed her Bessie was overwhelmed with a feeling she hadn't even known existed.

Step by step he seduced her. He was so subtle that she had no idea she was even being seduced. He would talk to her about conventions and how the common people needed rules to live by and flattered her and himself as being above the common rabble. It was his belief that a woman who gave herself to the man she loved was far more virtuous than one who teased and withheld herself until the man capitulated and married her. In his long conversations, he delicately led her down the primrose path until she was confused as to the difference between right and wrong, and good and evil; and by arousing in her a surprising and unsuspected passion.

He always stressed his great love and need for her, and one Sunday as they were walking along the bank of a gurgling stream he drew her down on the grassy bank in the shade of a leafy birch.

"Dearest Bessie," he said gently. "This must be my good-bye to you. I have been offered another station with better pay. God knows that I don't want to leave you, but it has got to the point where I can't stand to be with you any longer without claiming you for my own. It is best that I go away until I am financially able to ask for your hand in marriage."

The shock and devastation that overwhelmed Bessie left her devoid of words. Tears welled up in her eyes. This was a disaster of such enormity that suddenly a long empty life loomed before her.

Chauncey shrewdly pressed his suit without waiting for her to find her voice. He explained to her the great physical suffering that a man must endure when he was so deeply in love and could not claim the object of his affections.

She assured him that she didn't mind struggling to make ends meet when they were first married, but he brushed her protestations away. He was a proud man, Chauncey said, and he could not marry her until he could provide for her. "Darling," he begged with great feeling, "if you only loved me like I love you. Nothing could stand in the way, you'd come into my arms and really belong to me."

Bessie didn't want him to go away, and she didn't want him to suffer as he was so obviously doing. Torn between her deeply instilled training with lectures about all the terrible things that could happen to a girl who gave in to a man before they were married and the overweening passion that had grown between them, she let her love overcome her doubts.

Reluctantly, at the age of twenty, she relinquished her virginity. It was no sooner over than she bitterly regretted it. Almost instantly his attitude toward her changed. The act had been painful, and the necessity of washing herself in the stream was somehow ignoble with him looking on. She had made a grievous mistake and she knew it even though her love for him was undiminished. In the weeks after she had given herself to him she slipped quietly into his room at night at his behest and the lovemaking was marred by her fear of being discovered. But she seemed to have no will of her own.

She remembered those weeks after she had succumbed to Chauncey's will with shame, and she cringed when she thought of how stupid she had been. She worked hard to keep her love from spilling out for everyone to see. Chauncey was severe with her about any show of affection in public and became angry at anything that might be considered an infraction of the rule. He could treat her with a cold implacability that cut her to the heart. His slightest disapproving frown would bring tears to her eyes. The thought that he was spoiled and selfish never entered her head. She only knew that Chauncey, once he had his way with her, was quite different from the Chauncey who had worked so hard to win her.

How many times had she relived that terrible morning when she entered the dining room and saw that Chauncey was not in his usual place at the breakfast table. She was still tying her apron as she walked into the kitchen. Her mother was at the huge old iron cooking stove turning pancakes and breaking eggs into a pan as she talked to Faye, her youngest daughter. Bessie caught her right in the middle of a sentence.

". . . left early this morning. He tried to sneak out

without paying his back-board. When I caught him, he said he was sorry but he didn't have any money that he had sent it all to his wife and kids and he had to leave because of a family emergency. Said he'd send me the money soon's he got back on his feet. I don't believe that for a minute! He might have let us know he was married. All the time I thought he was real sweet on Bessie and something might come of it . . . "

She turned around with a platter of eggs and pancakes in her hands just in time to see Bessie crumple to the floor. When Bessie opened her eyes, she was on a couch in the parlor with Molly bending anxiously over her. The faces of her sister Faye and all seven of the boarders were swimming in the background.

She'll be fine now, go on back to your breakfast," she heard her mother saying from a great distance.

"Rich girls are always fainting and no one thinks a thing about it. I guess our Bessie is just putting on rich girl airs!" There was a little wave of laughter that seemed to relieve the tension and everyone trooped back to the table. Bessie knew that her mother wasn't nearly as flippant as she sounded as she turned back to her daughter.

There was worried concern in her voice as she said gently, "You fainted, honey, but I think you'll be just fine if you lie here and rest. Faye and I can manage. I think sometimes I work you too hard with you being so little and not very strong, but there is so much to do." Molly rested her hand on Bessie's head and for a moment their love was like a strong current pulsing between them. Bessie pulled her mother's hand to her lips and kissed it.

"I have to get back to the kitchen, honey, you just stay here and rest. I'll be back as soon as I get them all off to work."

Bessie put her hand over her mouth to muffle the cry of anguish that welled up inside her. If only her mother had been impatient with her for being so weak. She was shattered by her mother's love and concern. She knew only too well how hard her mother worked to pay the bills and keep her family together. Things hadn't been any better back when her father was home because the harder Molly worked, the harder her father drank and the more money he spent. Finally, after Faye was born, Molly had thrown Newton Hughes out and divorced him.

Bessie remembered how her father used to sing to her mother in his magnificent baritone, "Do you love me, Molly darlin'? "He was a fun loving, rollicking man in great demand because of his happy-go-lucky personality and his marvelous singing voice. Molly had adored the handsome Irishman when she married him, but years of trying to pay the rent and buy groceries when he came home on payday empty handed had cooled her ardor. He worked on the transcontinental railroad, and pay day meant stopping at the bar for a drink with the boys and then blowing every cent he made on booze for him and his free-loading friends. At first Molly had pleaded with him to change his ways and he would promise to bring her his next paycheck, but it never happened, and Molly was too proud to go down and collect it herself as some of the other women did. Gradually Molly's love turned to bitterness and then into something very like hate.

Now, Bessie thought sadly, she was about to heap more disappointment and responsibility on her mother's shoulders. Over a month had passed since she had told Chauncey she was in the family way. His first reaction was anger, and then he told her not to worry, they'd get married and everything would be fine. Just give him a little more time before they had to tell her mother.

Now he was gone and she was left to bear the consequences. She manufactured excuses for Chauncey, she told herself that it was all some dreadful mistake. Finally, because her mind could not accept the truth, she convinced herself that he would come back and that he'd marry her just as he had promised. He must have panicked at the thought of Molly's anger when she found out what had happened, and blurted out the first thing that came to mind. She knew that he couldn't possibly be married. Maybe he would send for her as soon as he found work. Bessie would give him time, and she wouldn't burden Molly with her problem, her eyes filled with tears at the thought of how she had betrayed her mother's trust.

Resolutely Bessie rose from the sofa, filled with strength and determination. She went back into the kitchen smiling reassuringly at her mother's protests.

The days flew by with Bessie clinging to her dreams and banishing any doubts that tried to push themselves into her consciousness by remembering how Chauncey had promised he'd take care of her and how they'd get married and everything would turn out fine.

It was late in November when Chauncey left, and the sound of a carriage stopping out in front of the boarding house on Elm Street would send her rushing to peer out from behind the parlor curtains her heart bounding wildly. Surely, she'd look out one time and it would be Chauncey coming back to her.

The months went by and as her body started to round out she remembered Molly looking at her approvingly and saying, "Bessie, you're putting on weight, and it's about time. You're beginning to look like a young woman instead of a scrawny little girl." It was true, in spite of the worry that was her daily companion, she knew that she was prettier than she had ever been. Her full shift-like dresses, her corset and her voluminous aprons hid her condition quite well.

March and April was only bearable because Molly's brother, Uncle Tobe, had moved in with them, and in the evenings when he wasn't playing checkers with her brother Jasper, she would get out her notebook and regale him with questions about the family. Uncle Tobe, as Charles Tobias Hess was called, knew everything about everyone on both sides of the family, and he loved to talk. Bessie had a secret desire to become a great writer like Charles Dickens or the Bronte sisters, and Uncle Tobe's stories were providing her with material for the Great American novel.

She had always thought that the rest of the family secretly laughed at her scribblings until the day she found Molly, tears sliding down her face, reading a poem Bessie had written.

"Oh, Bessie, it is so beautiful! I only wish I could send you to school to get the education you need." Then a bitter look crossed her face as she turned away, and Bessie knew her mother was thinking about Newton Hughes, and the anger in her heart that she harbored against him.

Molly had held up her head and tried so valiantly to maintain an aura of respectability even when Newton was flagrantly carrying on with another woman, and now, Bessie thought, the daughter she had been so proud of was about to bring disgrace to her family. Jasper, who was two years younger than she, was a lot wiser than she had been. Jasper disliked Chauncey from the start. He resented the superior air with which Chauncey regarded Bessie's family. Jasper had tried to warn her, Bessie thought sadly.

"How can you stand him?" he had asked her. "He thinks he's so much better than us and what's he? He's nothing but a railroad clerk."

Bessie was so smitten by Chauncey that she couldn't bear to hear him criticized and in the end, it drove a wedge between the closeness that she and Jasper had always shared.

Bessie blinked back her tears as she finally allowed herself to face the truth. Her face burned with shame when she recalled how Chauncey had once referred to her family as an uneducated bunch of clods and she had been too timid to defend them. Uneducated, she thought fiercely, but not clods. There was a dignity about Molly. She gave no quarter and she asked no quarter. There was no one who would have said that Molly was not a lady. She had never heard her mother swear and her grammar was far better than that of any of the other women she knew, but there was undeniably a certain toughness about Molly who thought any show of softness was an open invitation for someone to take advantage. Bessie smiled as she thought of the novels she had read and how in her mind the great lady who presided over her mansion with servants and all the trappings of the rich always looked exactly like Molly.

Molly was not beautiful, but she had a tremendous amount of personal magnetism. Men loved her and wanted her, but "once burned, twice shy". She had maintained her little family without the help of any man by dint of hard, back breaking, never ending work.

Faye, Bessie's youngest sister, was fifteen when Bessie was going through her travail. She was a tall well-built girl with blonde hair and large elongated blue eyes set in a strong face. Her mouth was wide and sensual and Molly worried about her disgracing the family. She was head strong, rebellious and bedazzled by a wild hard drinking young man named Otto Davis.

"I'm so worried that he'll get her in trouble," Molly confided to Bessie, and Bessie burdened with her guilty secret cringed. "If Faye marries him, she'll have the same kind of grief I had with Newton. It's no use talking to her, she won't listen. You and Iney have never given me a minute's trouble, nor Jasper either. I guess one out of the four of you had to take after your pa."

The stab of pain in Bessie's chest was as real as though a knife was twisting inside her. If only she had been more like Ina. Ina, the eldest of Molly's four children, was the most conventional. She married Mac Van Osdol when she was barely seventeen. He was twenty years her senior, but they were doing well and had presented Molly with her first grandchild, Darrel, who was over a year old.

Mac fell in love with Ina and married her. Why couldn't it have been like that with her and Chauncey? Of course, Bessie thought bitterly, no one could have talked Ina into entering into an illicit relationship. Why had she been born so weak willed? The whole family said that she just let people walk over her, and it was true. She had never been able to stand up for herself. Jasper had always defended her, and served as a buffer between her and any kind of adversity, but he hadn't been able to protect her against Chauncey.

Molly used to say that she understood the other three children, but she felt something like a mother hen that has hatched a duckling where Bessie was concerned. But there was pride in her voice as she went on to say that Bessie always had her nose in a book, and there wasn't anyone who could arrange a bowl of flowers or put a bow in just the right place on a dress like Bessie could.

It was late in April and it had rained daily all month. Sometimes misty droplets would fall steadily, and then again, buffeted by a wailing wind, the water would come down in great sheets spattering angrily on the street and battering against the window panes.

Bessie, Jasper and Uncle Tobe sat at the kitchen table with Molly sitting in her rocking chair, her lap overflowing with mending. The kitchen was filled with the spicy scent of the gingerbread Bessie had made early in the afternoon.

When Bessie looked over at Molly her heart contracted, how tired Molly looked. "Mama, are you all right?" Bessie asked anxiously. "You look so tired."

Molly smiled at her daughter. "It's a good kind of tired, Bessie. I was just thinking how good things have been going. I paid up the grocery bill today and we're finally even, the mortgage payments are up to date, and we're all well. I guess a body can't ask more'n that. Just sitting here with all of you and listening to the rain beat on the roof that's almost mine makes me thankful. I'll have the dratted mortgage all paid off in a few months." Molly added proudly. "We're better off than a lot of folks."

Bessie turned away from her mother's loving gaze, unable to face her. "I'm sorry Uncle Tobe, I didn't mean to interrupt you." she said, her voice almost inaudible. Bessie had been listening with rapt attention as Tobe retold the saga of the Bryants and the Hesses.

"I don't mind givin' someone else a chance to get a word in edgeways," said Uncle Tobe, "and besides I wanted to tell you that you look mighty pretty sitting there with the light shining on your hair."

"I was thinking the same thing," said Jasper. He was sprawled out over his chair, listening, with his hands in his pockets, and an enigmatic look on his face.

"The Bryants came from Ireland" Tobe was saying. "They came up from the South on one of the early wagon trains. The Hesses came from Virginia. There was some talk that they were Jews who couldn't make it back there because of the prejudice. They never seemed to have a religion, maybe that's why people thought they were Jews. I doubt if grandpa Hughes was, but I wouldn't be surprised if grandmother was a Jewess. The two wagon trains came out at about the same time but from different places so the two families never met until they settled near Newburg, Oregon. Our families founded the town, you know. Your grandfather, John Hess, has the distinction of being the first white child born in the state of Oregon as you've been told enough times."

"I never get tired of hearing about them," Bessie murmured. She shifted her position in the hard kitchen chair. Her back had been giving her fits for nearly a week. She wondered fleetingly how much longer she could keep her secret, so far, she had just rounded out instead of bulging out in front as was the usual case with women in the family way.   Please, please, Chauncey, she whispered silently, you can't leave me to face all this alone. She tore her thoughts away from the problem for which there was no solution.

"Nobody knows exactly what the reason was, but the Bryants and the Hughes' were mortal enemies," Uncle Tobe was saying. "There was a lot of fighting and some bloodshed. Some people say it was over religion. The Bryants were strict Irish Catholics and they thought that anyone who believed different was a heathen and they didn't mind saying so. Others said it had to do with disagreements over land. Whatever the reason, they hated each other, and that went along for almost a generation until your great grandmother, Mary Bryant, eloped on horseback with your great grandfather, John Hess. After that the feud sort of died out."

"My grandma, Mary Bryant, was alive when I was a youngster and she used to tell about the trip by covered wagon into Oregon, and how coming across the plains the children had to gather buffalo chips to build the cooking fires. They nearly froze to death in the mountains, and almost starved to boot. A lot of them died. I guess when you think about it we come from a hardy line of people and we can be proud of it. I didn't know my other grandmother as well. Her name was Rachel and she was a proud, distant sort of lady. The story was that she came from a family of wealth in the old country. You never could get her to talk about it or how she happened to marry grandpa. My mother used to say it was like a plow horse and a race horse trying to pull the same wagon. We were all a little scared of her and we always addressed her as grandmother.

She never really made friends with the other pioneer women and seemed as though she thought she was better than them. She was good with children and made it her business to teach as many of them as she could to read. I guess you might say she was kind of a born teacher. She knew a great deal about cooking and taught the other women a lot about herbs and roots. She gave them recipes for things they'd never even heard of, like beet soup and stuffed cabbage leaves. Her real fame was as a midwife. She saved many a baby that had trouble getting into the world. Men came from miles around to get her when their wives were having a difficult labor. If Rachel couldn't save the baby, no one could. People looked up to her, but nobody ever got close to her."

"It's hard for me to try to picture what those people went through trying to carve a home out of the wilderness," Tobe said thoughtfully, "It must be well-nigh impossible for you young folks used to all these modern conveniences, gas lights, trolley cars and a kitchen sink with a pump so you can pump water right from the well. Your grandma had to tote water from the river for her cooking and washed her clothes in the river. Life in those days was hard on women all but the hardiest died young."

"I can't see that it has changed a lot," Jasper cut in. He so seldom made an observation, that they all looked at him in surprise. "Look at Ma, worked and slaved all her life for what? Tell you one thing, I'm never going to get married and put some poor girl through all this. There isn't any way I'm ever going to make a decent living and I know it. A Few people got it all and the rest of us poor suckers'll break our backs to the grave and end up with nothing."

"Why Jasper," Molly said bewildered, "I never knew you felt that way." Molly looked over at Bessie, and her eyes widened with shock. The lamp cast a path of light across the floor and in its glow Molly saw Bessie had suddenly bent forward, her face contorted in agony. A rivulet of water formed into a puddle on the floor by Bessie's chair. For the first time in her life Molly was frozen in the face of an emergency, she simply could not collect her wits.

It was Jasper who sprang to Bessie's side and was giving terse quick commands, sending Tobe to get Doc Fisher and carrying the ashen faced Bessie into the bedroom off the kitchen where he laid her gently on the bed.

"I think Bessie is about to give birth," Jasper said quietly. "What? gasped Molly. "How can that be? She never even...she doesn't look..."

Jasper's face was ravaged as he looked at his mother, "I've suspected it for some time. Bessie hasn't been right since that scum Chauncey left. And her fillin' out like she has, well, something had to be wrong."

"Oh, my God, Jasper, why didn't you say something? Why didn't I see it? How could she have gone through this and me not even suspecting?" Molly made a Herculean effort to pull herself together. As Bessie lay stretched flat on the bed Molly was aware for the first time of the rising roundness of her abdomen.

Bessie could never quite recall all that happened in that next hour. She was gripped in such spasms of agony that the room seemed to expand and recede with everything unreal but the pain. The doctor had arrived and within thirty minutes he handed Molly the tiniest human being she had ever seen.

"This baby is nowhere near term, probably six and a half to seven months, not any more. Be a miracle if it lives or if we can save Bessie either." The old doctor was talking as he moved swiftly. "Jasper you'll have to do the best you can for the baby. Get a hand towel and wrap her up. Keep her warm. That's about all we can do now. Molly, we've got work to do."

Bessie heard them talking as though she was a wraith hovering above all that was going on in the room. She was hemorrhaging and the doctor had instructed Molly in how to place her hand on the outside of Bessie's abdomen to hold the writhing uterus.

It was finally over and the doctor was wrapping Bessie in a tight binder. He looked tired. "I don't know who did this to Bessie, but I'd like to see him horsewhipped. I brought all your children into the world, but I always had a special soft spot for little Bessie and you know it." His voice sharpened. "Don't you think you could have told me what was going on?"

"I don't know if you'll believe this," Molly said miserably, "But I swear I never even suspected she was in the family way. I just thought she was getting plump after all these years of being so skinny."

He looked keenly at Molly for a moment. "I guess you didn't, Molly. Your children never struck me as being afraid of you. Why do you suppose she didn't tell you? Molly shook her head mutely. The doctor went on talking.

"Can you imagine what this poor child has gone through?"

Bessie heard them talking and she wanted them to know that she wasn't asleep, but she was too weak to make any sign.

"She may not pull through, Molly, she's lost a way more blood than she can afford to. Whether she pulls through or not may depend on you. She's got to want to live, and she's going to be worrying about the disgrace and all that claptrap. She needs to know that you love her in spite of what has happened. The child came way too fast and Bessie is pretty badly torn. It's not likely she'll ever have another child. If this one lives it will be a miracle. You never know about babies, though. If the little tyke's a scrapper... well, who knows? We'll just have to do what we can. "

The doctor was washing his hands in the basin that Molly had provided for him as he talked. "I've done about all I can for her, and now we'd better take a look at the baby."

Bessie heard later about how they found Jasper in the warm, lamp lit kitchen, and how the doctor smiled as he spied the shoe box setting on a kitchen chair near the open oven door. On closer inspection, he saw that the box was lined with carded lamb's wool and the infant wrapped in what looked like a dish towel was tucked inside. Carefully the old doctor lifted the child out of her nest and laid her on the kitchen table so he could examine her. A tiny wail of protest came from the baby girl.

"Jasper, you've done a mighty good job," Doc said with approval, "Got her all cleaned up, too!"

"Jasper, would have made a wonderful doctor," Molly murmured.

The doctor was gently prodding, and moving little arms and legs as he inspected the child. "Fingers and toes all here, head a mite big," It was almost as though he was talking to himself. "Liver enlarged, might have trouble with jaundice, lungs as clear as could be expected, heart beat weak." He tended to the umbilical cord and tore a towel to make a binder. Molly marveled at his sure and quick efficiency. He took a scale from his black bag. It had a hook on the end of it and he carried a triangular cloth with a knot that fitted over the hook so he could slip a baby into the cloth hammock.

"I don't know if it's important enough to disturb her, but I would like to know just how much she weighs." Doctor Fisher said. "My God, Molly," he exclaimed. "She doesn't even weigh four pounds! It's going to take some doing to pull this little mite through! You've got your work cut out for you, Molly Hughes." He tucked the baby back into its shoe box, talking rapidly as he gave Molly instructions.
Then they went in to check on Bessie.

Bessie was aware that Jasper was sitting beside her and that his tears were falling on her hands as he held them tightly in his. She was in a state of euphoria such as she had never known. Her pain was gone and she felt as though she were floating.

"She is so weak, Maw," he said brokenly, "and she says she is dying. Maw, don't let our Bessie go." Jasper was overcome with grief and started to sob with his shoulders shaking convulsively.

Suddenly Molly was filled with an all-consuming anger. She shook Bessie until her eyes opened. "You look here, Bessie Hughes," she grated. "I don't want to hear any talk about you dying." She gave her a little shake. "You're not going to leave me with a baby to care for, I've raised enough young'uns. It'd be real easy for you to just close your eyes and step out of this world and leave the picking up of the pieces to the rest of us. Well, you're not going to do it. Do you hear me!" Molly's anger flashed like daggers from her dark blue eyes. She literally forced Bessie to struggle back from the welcoming arms of death.

Molly went on, but her tone was kinder. "Maybe you think we don't want you any more, Bessie. Well, we may not be much but we stand by our own, and maybe you made a mistake but that doesn't make us love you any the less. We're going to hold up our heads and we'll get through this. Tongues will wag for a while, but people got their own lives to live and their own troubles. I don't want to hear any more talk about dying, do you understand?" Bessie nodded weakly.

Molly bent down and kissed her. "You're my little girl, Bessie, and maybe I've been too busy to show it, but I love you and it would tear my heart out to lose you."

Bessie's tears started to fall, making the pillow wet as Molly talked, and Molly knew that she had won. Bessie would make the heroic effort necessary to live.

Doctor Fisher sat down on a chair by the bed. "Well, young lady, I think you're going to pull through now. He was listening to her heart. What you need is a lot of good nourishing food and rest. Now, what was that fellow's name, again?" he asked Molly. He had taken some papers out of his bag and Molly watched as he scratched out the date, April 20, 1910. He looked up at her expectantly, and when she answered he filled out the birth certificate with the father's name, Chauncey Miller, and Bessie's name, and wrote legitimate in the proper space.

"I didn't know you could do that," Molly breathed.

"I can do anything I've a mind to," Doc Fisher said sharply, and I don't think there is such a thing as an illegitimate baby. So far nobody has ever questioned me, but if they want to put me in jail they can."

Bessie heard them talking in the kitchen, and her heart swelled with gratitude as she thought of the kind old doctor who with a stroke of his pen had made her daughter legitimate. He was checking the baby again as he gave Molly last minute instructions

"It's early to tell for sure, but the baby's breathing better than I expected. We're going to have to feed her with an eye dropper until she is strong enough to suck. I don't want Bessie's milk to dry up after it comes in even if you have to borrow a baby to stimulate it."

Bessie raised up weakly on her pillow as she heard Molly start to sob, she had never in her life seen or heard the indomitable Molly cry. Her mother's muffled voice came to Bessie with each word cutting into her soul.

"Oh, Doc, I know a lot of this was my fault. I should have known what that smooth-talking reprobate was up to. Bessie's a good girl, I know that, and now her life is ruined. Oh God, I could kill him."

"Molly, her life is not ruined," the Doctor answered sharply, "you have to get that out of your head. It's only ruined if you let it be, where's your pride?" Bessie could see them in her mind's eye with his arm around Molly, patting her shoulder.

"You may not know it, Molly girl, but you saved her life in there, she was slipping away and you dragged her back just as surely as I'm standing here. Bessie is a whole head above most of the girls I know, she can come through all this if she knows she's loved. I just hope this baby survives because I doubt if Bessie will ever have another one."

"You know, Doc, something's been bothering me, and it just came to me. You asked me why Bessie didn't tell me. I think I know now. She always worries because I have to work so hard and have so much on my mind, I guess she couldn't bear to add to my worries. She probably thought that-that scum, that creature, would come back and marry her. Poor little thing," and Molly started to cry again.

"It's not fair, Molly," Doc Fisher said. "I see a lot of women in my business and the things that men do to them!   I don't have too much respect for some of the members of my own sex."

CHAPTER 17

Bessie awakened with a shock, she was stiff and cramped from sleeping on the swing and the darkness of the night had melted into a soft gray. She looked up at the waning stars and made up her mind that she would survive all this and that somehow, sometime she'd be a credit to her mother. Even as she made her vow a feeling of futility swept over her and a bitter smile moved fleetingly across her face.

Here she was again dreaming dreams that would never come to be. No matter what lofty resolutions she might make, her mistakes had hurt everyone, including herself. There was no way they could be undone, and no way she could change things. She was tied to a man whom she had difficulty in even liking, let alone loving. She was about to bear another child and she'd have to relinquish it as soon as it was born. It would be legitimate, according to the law. George Stange would be the registered father. She pulled herself up. Somehow everything she did turned out wrong. She couldn't even die in peace because there'd be no one to care for Doris. She allowed herself a ghost of a smile, at least she had finally brought herself around to facing the facts.

She pulled herself to her feet by holding on to the swing for support and then made her way into the kitchen. Unexpectedly a sharp pain ripped through her as she started to fill the teakettle with water. She staggered and reached for a chair back for support. She struggled to keep from losing consciousness as another pain ripped through her insides and tore through her body. The world was turning topsy-turvy and an ocean of blackness was sweeping her away.

164

CHAPTER 18

Early the following, Molly was awakened by a pounding on the door. It was George and he looked so distraught that Molly's heart almost stopped in her breast

"She ain't dead yet," said George, thinking that this bit of news would be comforting to Molly. "Doc is with Bessie and they sent me to get you."

On the way George told her about finding Bessie on the kitchen floor early in the morning.

"A while she was unconscious. My God, Molly I thought she was dead, but when I picked her up in my arms and carried her back to bed she came to. She seemed to be all right then, wasn't in no pain, said the water had broken and no need to call the doctor for a while. She went to sleep then and slept to near noon. I was clear out of my mind, not wanting to leave her alone and not knowin' whether to wake her up or let her sleep. Finally, she woke up and one of them terrible pains came that seemed like it might tear her apart.

"I kept hopin' you or Faye would come by. Livin' out like we do I was afraid to leave her to get help." He turned his haggard face to Molly. "I was near crazy, and Dorse kept whining and wanting her mama to get up. Well, that went on until near six o'clock in the evening and those pains kept comin' and goin' every forty-five minutes or so and she was gettin' weaker and weaker so there wasn't nothin' left but to grab up Dorse and leave Bessie alone while I went to get help. Doc sent Dora Smithers back with me to help out 'til he could get there. When I said every forty-five minutes those pains was comin', I guess he didn't realize how terrible they was, or he'd of gotten there right off."

At six o'clock that morning, August 23, l913, exhausted and nearly dead from loss of blood, Bessie delivered a fourand-a-half-pound baby girl who was registered as Baby Stange.

Molly took the baby home with her and two days later she put the child in Lew's arms. Remembering the dream he'd had, Lew turned the blanket back and looked into the wrinkled little face of his daughter. The baby stared back at her father with grave blue eyes and Lew could never forget the flash of recognition that came over him. It was as though in some other time and some other place their lives had been joined together.

9 781986 207836